CROCHET
GARMENTS

15 STUNNING PROJECTS TO CREATE A
FASHIONABLE WARDROBE

CARRIE CHAMBERS

Tuva Publishing
www.tuvapublishing.com

Address Merkez Mah. Cavusbasi Cad. No.71
Cekmekoy - Istanbul 34782 / Türkiye
Tel +9 0216 642 62 62

Crochet Garments

First Print 2025 / July

All Global Copyrights Belong to
Tuva Tekstil ve Yayıncılık Ltd.

Content Crochet

Editor in Chief Ayhan DEMİRPEHLİVAN
Project Editor Kader DEMİRPEHLİVAN
Author Carrie CHAMBERS
Technical Editors Cherie MELLICK, Leyla ARAS
Graphic Designers Ömer ALP, Abdullah BAYRAKÇI, Tarık TOKGÖZ, Yunus GÜLDOĞAN
Photography Carrie CHAMBERS, Tuva Publishing

All rights are reserved. No part of this publication may be reproduced, stored in a retrieval system, or transmitted in any form or by any means, electronic, mechanical, photocopying, recording, or otherwise, without prior written consent of the publisher. The copyrights of the designs in this book are protected and may not be used for any commercial purpose.

ISBN 978-605-7834-72-0

The EEA authorised representative is Authorised Rep Compliance Ltd. Ground Floor, 71 Lower Baggot Street, Dublin, DO2 P593, Ireland (www.arccompliance.com)

 TuvaPublishing

ACKNOWLEDGEMENTS

I would like to express my deepest gratitude to my beautiful daughter, Sophia, who has been with me every step of the way throughout my crochet journey. From the beginning, she has been my constant source of support, always willing to model my crochet creations without ever complaining. She truly is my everything, and I love her more than words can ever convey.

A heartfelt thank you goes to my partner, Martin, who has stood by my side through both the great and challenging moments. His unwavering belief in me and his encouragement have been invaluable, especially during the times when I doubted my ability. He cheered me on and reminded me of my passion, which kept me motivated.

I am also immensely grateful to Kader and Tuva Publishing for believing in me and reaching out with the opportunity to write this book. It still amazes me that they saw something in my work and wanted this collaboration. I will be forever grateful.

Finally, I want to thank everyone who follows me online and supports my craft. Your encouragement has transformed my life in ways you may never fully understand, and for that, I thank you from the bottom of my heart.

Love,

Carrie

CONTENTS

INTRODUCTION..................................4

MATERIALS AND TOOLS......................8

CROCHET STITCHES.........................10

PROJECTS

Ardmore Texture Cardigan..................16

Cashel Cardigan................................22

Cleggan Crew Neck Sweater..............26

Connemara Pocket Shawl..................32

Elly Bobble Cardigan.........................36

Fanore Sweater Scarf........................42

Fawnmore Ribbed Cardigan..............46

Foxford V Neck Sweater....................52

Kingstown Sweater Vest....................58

Newbridge Turtleneck Slipover........64

Newport Top Down Sweater..............70

Omey Puffy Sweater..........................76

Roundstone Cocoon Shrug................82

Mulranny Sweater.............................86

Sycamore Hooded Gilet.....................90

INTRODUCTION

When I was a child in school, I first tried to learn crochet but found it frustrating and difficult at the time. It wasn't until many years later when I revisited the craft, this time learning through YouTube tutorials, that I began my journey with crochet. With patience and determination, I not only mastered the art, but I also fell deeply in love with it. Inspired by my own learning journey, I decided to start my own YouTube channel. I focused on designing sweaters, cardigans, hats and other garments, all of which helped me build a large and supportive following. As my love for crochet grew, I expanded in writing patterns and launched my blog, **www.crochetwithcarrie.com**, which has become a popular resource for crocheters of all levels. When it comes to designing, I love creating garments that are full of texture, giving each piece a unique and dynamic look. Sometimes I enjoy experimenting with certain designs that mimic the look and feel of knitwear, pushing the boundaries of what crochet can achieve.

In this book you'll find a variety of crochet patterns, including shawls, sweaters, cardigans, vests and tops. Each design is filled with texture and style, from simple, elegant pieces to more intricate garments. This book includes patterns for all skill levels, from beginners to more advanced crocheters, so there's definitely something for everyone to enjoy.

Writing a book has been a dream of mine since I was a child and I'm so excited to finally share my designs in this way. I want to thank everyone who has supported me online, followed my tutorials and enjoyed making garments from my patterns. Your encouragement and creativity inspire me every day and I hope the patterns in this book inspire you to create something amazing.

Happy crocheting,

Carrie

PROJECT GALLERY

15 STUNNING PROJECTS TO CREATE A FASHIONABLE WARDROBE

P.16

P.22

P.26

P.32

P.36

P.42

MATERIALS AND TOOLS

YARN

Throughout this book I have used different brands, yarn weights and fibers for each pattern. Each yarn listed is simply a suggestion however if you wish to make your garment in a different yarn there are a few rules you must abide by. Firstly be sure that your substitute yarn works to the same gauge listed in the pattern. Failure to do so will cause major problems down the line, problems you can certainly do without! Secondly, it is best to choose a yarn with a similar fiber content as this can seriously affect the look and drape of a garment. Finally, take time choosing your yarn. The color and feel of your chosen yarn will make a huge impact to your finished garment. After all, the item you make will hopefully be something you will wear and cherish for many years to come.

CROCHET HOOK

Crochet hooks come in various sizes and materials like metal, plastic or wood, each suited to different types of yarn and projects. Use the hook size that is stated in the pattern, making sure to check your tension. If you find you have more stitches in your swatch than the stated gauge, opt for a larger hook. If you have fewer stitches then use a smaller hook.

HOOK SIZE CONVERSION CHART

Metric	Imperial (UK & Canada)	US
2mm	14	-
2.25mm	13	B-1
2.5mm	12	-
2.75mm	-	C-2
3mm	11	-
3.25mm	10	D-3
3.5mm	9	E-4
3.75mm	-	F-5
4mm	8	G-6
4.5mm	7	7
5mm	6	H-8
5.5mm	5	I-9
6mm	4	J-10
6.5mm	3	K-10 ½
7mm	2	-
8mm	0	L-11
9mm	00	M/N-13
10mm	000	N/P-15

TENSION/GAUGE

Gauge plays a critical role not only in crochet. It can be influenced by factors like hook size, yarn weight and personal tension. Even experienced crocheters can vary in their tension, which is why testing a gauge swatch – a small sample of crochet work- is important. If the gauge is too tight, switching to a larger hook may correct it, while a smaller hook can adjust a loose gauge. Ignoring gauge can lead to ill-fitting garments, running out of yarn before completion, and a whole lot of heartache.

Making a 4x4" swatch in crochet is important because it helps you accurately check your gauge before starting a project. This swatch provides a large enough sample to give an accurate representation of how your tension works with the yarn and hook you are using.

The swatch allows you to compare your stitch and row count to a pattern's specified gauge. If your swatch has too many or too few stitches (or rows) within the 4x4" swatch your project may end up too small or too large.

BLOCKING

Blocking is an essential finishing step in crochet that helps projects achieve their final shape, size and drape. By stretching and pinning your crochet project to a specific shape and size, you can even out stitches, smooth out uneven edges and open up intricate stitch patterns.

There are three main types of blocking:

1. Wet blocking: This involves soaking the crochet piece in water, gently squeezing out excess moisture and pinning it to the desired shape on blocking mat. It's ideal for natural fibers like wool, which respond well to moisture.

2. Steam blocking: This method uses steam from an iron or steamer to shape the project. Hold the steam above the fabric without touching it, then pin in place. Its works well for synthetic fibers or blends.

3. Spray blocking: For this, you lightly spray the project with water, then shape and pin it. This way is a lot gentler and perfect for delicate fibers.

SEAMING METHODS

Seaming or joining methods in crochet are essential for projects that involves multiple pieces. There are several common techniques to seam a crochet sweater together, each offering different finishes:

The whip stitch is a simple sewing technique that creates an invisible seam, often used on the wrong side of the fabric. Slip stitch seaming is another method that uses a crochet hook to join pieces, creating a sturdy, flat seam. Finally, the mattress stitch which offers a near invisible seam, perfect for garments where neatness is of utmost importance. Play around with the method that suits you best.

WEAVING IN ENDS

Weaving in ends is an important finishing step in crochet garments to ensure a clean, polished look and lasting durability. When you add a new ball of yarn or finish sections, loose ends are left behind. If not properly woven in, these ends can unravel over time, leading to a messy appearance or even damaging the garment. Weaving in the ends securely not only prevents fraying but also keeps the edges neat and tidy.

It's best to weave ends in different directions through several stitches, blending them in the texture of the project. This creates a seamless, invisible finish while maintaining the garment's integrity and ensuring it holds up through wear and tear.

CROCHET STITCHES

Slip Knot

Make a loop with your yarn, insert the hook through the loop and pick up the ball end of the yarn, draw through loop and pull in tail end gently.

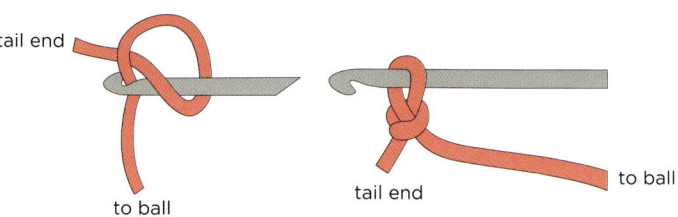

Yarn Over (yo)

Wrap the yarn from back to front around your hook.

Chain (ch)

Start with a slip knot or loop on the hook, yo and pull through the loop on your hook*. To work more chain stitches repeat from * to *.

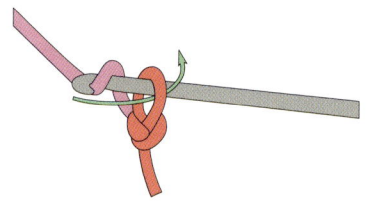

Single Crochet (sc)

Insert hook into stitch or space indicated, yo and draw up a loop, (2 loops on hook), yo and pull through both loops to complete the stitch.

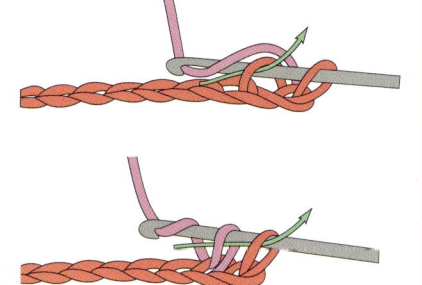

Half Double Crochet (hdc)

Yo, insert hook into stitch or space indicated, yo and draw up a loop, (3 loops on hook), yo and draw through all three loops to complete the stitch.

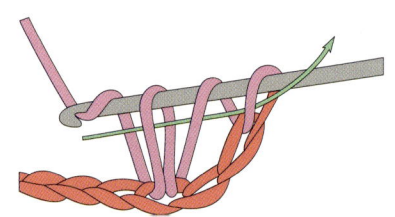

Double Crochet (dc)

Yo, insert hook into stitch or space indicated, yo and draw up a loop (3 loops on hook), yo and draw through two loops, yo and draw through next two loops to complete the stitch.

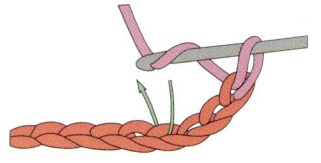
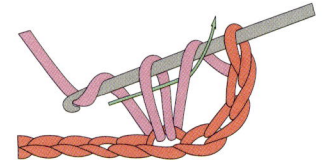

Treble Crochet (tr)

Wrap yarn twice around hook, insert hook into stitch or space indicated, yo and draw up a loop, (4 loops on hook), yo and draw through 2 loops; repeat from * twice more to complete the stitch.

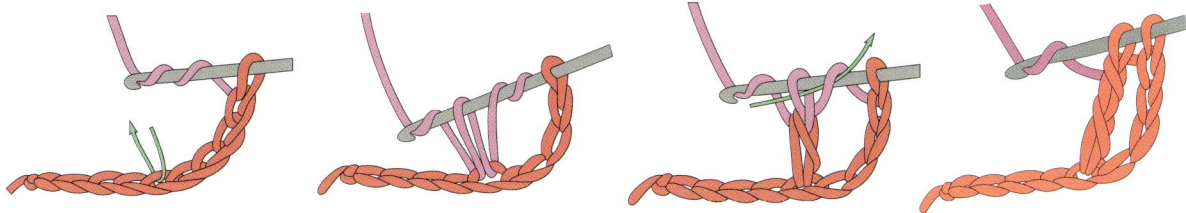

Slip Stitch (sl st)

Insert hook into stitch or space indicated, yo and draw up a loop, pull this new loop through the loop on your hook to complete the stitch.

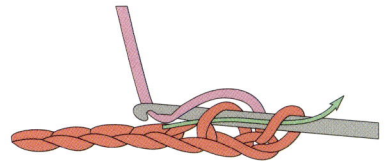

Back Loop Only (blo)

Insert hook into back part of stitch only (ie the back part of the 'V' looking down on the stitch from the top.

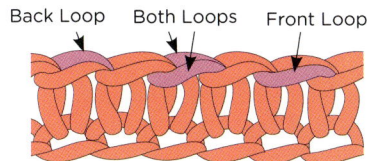

Puff (ps)

Yo, insert hook in stitch or space indicated, yo and pull up a loop to height of 1 dc; repeat from * twice more, (7 loops on hook), yo, pull through all 7 loops, ch1 to complete the stitch.

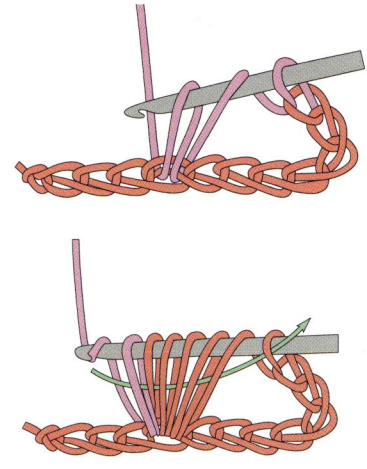

Front Post Double Crochet (FPdc)

Yo, insert hook from front to back to front around vertical post of next stitch, yo and draw up a loop, (3 loops on hook), yo and draw through two loops, yo and draw through next two loops to complete the stitch.

Back Post Double Crochet (BPdc)

Yo, insert hook from back to front to back around vertical post of next stitch, yo and draw up a loop, (3 loops on hook), Yo and draw through two loops, yo and draw through next two loops to complete the stitch.

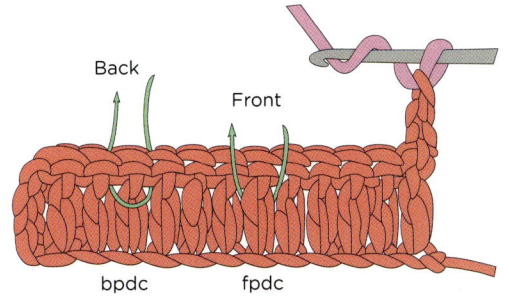

Single Crochet 2 Together (sc2tog)

Insert the hook into the first stitch, yo and pull up a loop. Then insert hook in next stitch, yo and pull up a loop. (3 loops on hook). yo, pull through all 3 loops.

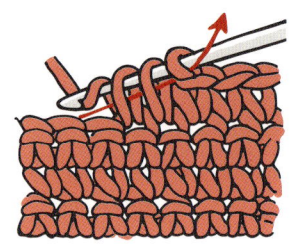 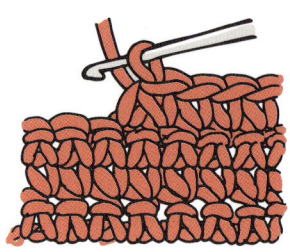

Half Double Crochet 2 Together (hdc2tog)

Yo, insert hook into the first stitch, yo and pull up a loop. Then yo, insert hook into the next stitch, yo and pull up a loop. (5 loops on hook). yo, pull through all 5 loops.

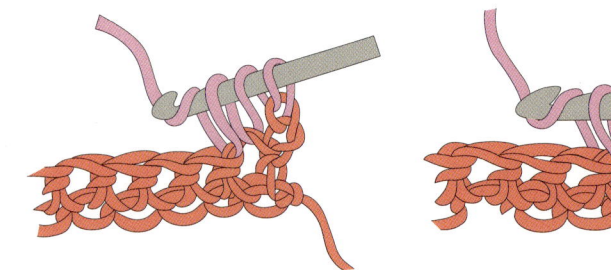 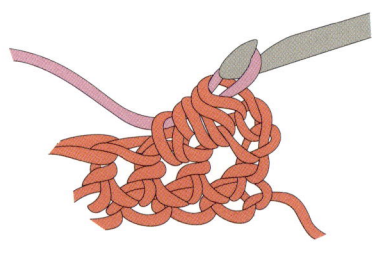

Herringbone Half Double Crochet

Yo, insert hook into stitch or space indicated, yo and draw up a loop (3 loops on hook), pull new loop through one loop on hook, yo, draw through two loops on hook.

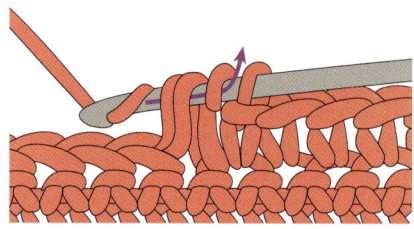

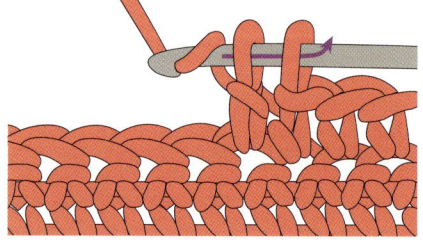

Herringbone Half Double Crochet Decrease

Yo, insert hook into stitch or space indicated , yo and draw up a loop (3 loops on hook), pull new loop through one loop on hook, yo, insert hook into next stitch, yo and draw up a loop (4 loops on hook), pull new loop through one loop on hook, yo, draw through three loops on hook.

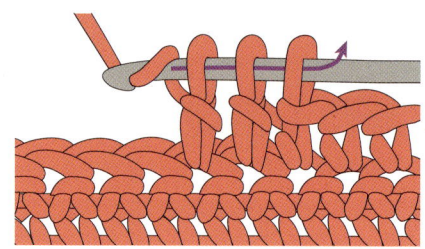

PROJECTS

ARDMORE
TEXTURE CARDIGAN

Slightly cropped and featuring an intricate almond stitch texture throughout, creating a rich, tactile feel. Its cropped silhouette adds a modern touch, while the textured pattern brings depth and dimension. This versatile cardigan combines classic elegance with contemporary style, perfect for both casual and dressy occasions.

SKILL LEVEL
Intermediate

LIST OF MATERIALS
Drops, Lima – Chestnut
1 ¾ oz, 109 yds / 50 g, 100 m
14 [14, 15, 15, 16, 17] balls

Size H-8 (5 mm) hook

Stitch Marker

Tapestry Needle

GAUGE
17 sts = 4" (10 cm); 19 rows = 4" (10 cm)

ABBREVIATIONS
ch: chain
hdc: half double crochet
sl st: slip stitch
st(s): stitch(es)

SIZING

Instructions given for Small, with changes for Medium, Large, XL, 2XL, 3XL are in [ ].

SIZE	S	M	L	XL	2XL	3XL
Finished Bust	40" 107 cm	44" 112 cm	48" 122 cm	52" 132 cm	56" 142 cm	60" 152.5 cm
Total Length	22" 56 cm	22" 56 cm	23" 58 cm	23" 58 cm	24" 61 cm	24" 61 cm
Arm Circumference	15" 38 cm	16" 41 cm	16" 41 cm	17" 43 cm	17" 43 cm	18" 46 cm

Pattern Notes

Ch 1 at beginning of row does NOT count as first stitch.

FIRST FRONT PANEL

Ch 85 [85, 85, 93, 93, 93]

Row 1: Sl st in second ch from hook and in each of next 3 ch, *hdc in each of next 4 ch, sl st in each of next 4 ch; repeat from * across, turn. (84 [84, 84, 92, 92, 92] sts)

Row 2: Ch 1; working in **back loops** only, sl st in each of next 4 sts; *working in **back loops** only, hdc in each of next 4 sts; working in **back loops** only, sl st in each of next 4 sts; repeat from * across, turn.

Row 3: Ch 1; working in **back loops** only, hdc in each of next 4 sts; *working in **back loops** only, sl st in each of next 4 sts; working in **back loops** only, hdc in each of next 4 sts; repeat from * across, turn.

Row 4: Repeat Row 3.

Repeat Rows 1-4 until you have completed a total of 36 [40, 44, 48, 52, 56] rows. Do NOT fasten off. Continue to Back Panel.

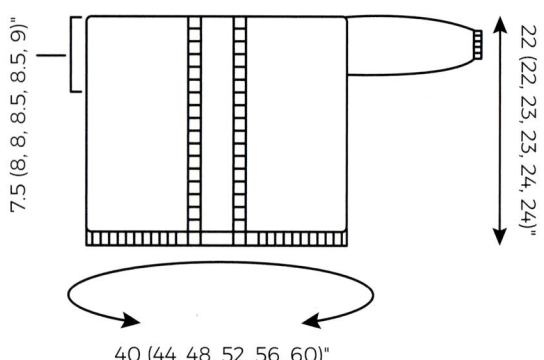

BACK PANEL

Row 1: Ch 1; working in **back loops** only, sl st in each of next 4 sts; *working in **back loops** only, hdc in each of next 4 sts; working in **back loops** only, sl st in each of next 4 sts; repeat from * across a total of 24 [23, 23, 26, 26, 25] times leaving remaining 32 [34, 34, 36, 36, 38] sts unworked, turn.

Row 2: Ch 33 [35, 35, 37, 37, 39], sl st in second ch from hook and in each of next 3 ch, [hdc in each of next 4 ch, sl st in each of next 4 ch] 14 [15, 15, 16, 16, 17] times; *working in **back loops** only, hdc in each of next 4 sts; sl st in each of next 4 sts; repeat from * across, turn.

Rows 3-4: *(2 rows)* Ch 1; working in **back loops** only, hdc in each of next 4 sts; *working in **back loops** only, sl st in each of next 4 sts; working in **back loops** only, hdc in each of next 4 sts; repeat from * across, turn.

Rows 5-6: *(2 rows)* Ch 1; working in **back loops** only, sl st in each of next 4 sts; *working in **back loops** only, hdc in each of next 4 sts; working in **back loops** only, sl st in each of next 4 sts; repeat from * across, turn.

Repeat Rows 3-6 until you have completed a total of 94 [102, 114, 122, 130, 142] rows. Do NOT fasten off. Continue to Second Front Panel.

SECOND FRONT PANEL

Row 1: Ch 1; working in **back loops** only, hdc in each of next 4 sts; *working in **back loops** only, sl st in each of next 4 sts; working in **back loops** only, hdc in each of next 4 sts; repeat from * across a total of 24 [23, 23, 26, 26, 25] times leaving remaining 32 [34, 34, 36, 36, 38] sts unworked, turn.

Row 2: Hdc in second ch from hook and in each of next 3 ch, [sl st in each of next 4 ch, hdc in each of next 4 ch] 14 [15, 15, 16, 16, 17] times; *working in **back loops** only, sl st in each of next 4 sts; working in **back**

loops only, hdc in each of next 4 sts; repeat from * across, turn.

Row 3: Ch 1; working in back loops only, sl st in each of next 4 sts; *working in back loops only, hdc in each of next 4 sts; working in back loops only, sl st in each of next 4 sts; repeat from * across, turn.

Row 4: Repeat Row 3.

Rows 5-6: (2 rows) Repeat Row 2.

Rows 7-8: (2 rows) Repeat Row 3.

Repeat Rows 5-8 until you have completed a total of 36 [40, 44, 48, 52, 56] rows. Fasten off.

SLEEVES (Make 2)

Ch 77

Row 1: Sl st in second ch from hook and in each of next 3 ch, *hdc in each of next 4 ch, sl st in each of next 4 ch; repeat from * across until 8 sts remain, sl st in each of next 8 ch, turn. (76 sts)

Row 2: Ch 1; working in back loops only, sl st in each of next 12 sts; *working in back loops only, hdc in each of next 4 sts; repeat from * across, turn.

Row 3: Ch 1; working in back loops only, sl st in each of next 4 sts; *working in back loops only, hdc in each of next 4 sts; working in back loops only, sl st in each of next 4 sts; repeat from * across until 8 sts remain; working in back loops only, sl st in each of next 8 sts, turn.

Row 4: Ch 1; working in back loops only, sl st in each of next 8 sts; working in back loops only, hdc in each of next 4 sts; *working in back loops only, sl st in each of next 4 sts, working in back loops only, hdc in each of next 4 sts ; repeat from * across, turn.

Row 5: Ch 1; working in back loops only, sl st in each of next 4 sts; *working in back loops only, hdc in each of next 4 sts; working in back loops only, sl st in each of next 4 sts; repeat from * across until 8 sts remain; working in back loops only, sl st in each of next 8 sts, turn.

Row 6: Repeat Row 2.

Repeat Rows 3-6 until you have completed a total of 70 [74, 74, 78, 78, 82] rows. Fasten off, leaving a long tail for seaming. Fold fabric in half lengthwise, so the edges line up. Using tapestry needle and tail, seam the edges together.

ASSEMBLY

Joining Panels

With right sides touching, lay the front panels on back panel, lining row ends at shoulder seam. Using tapestry needle and tail, seam the shoulders together using a whip stitch.

Joining Sleeves

Align sleeves with armhole of body. Using a tapestry needle and tail, seam through both layers to join.

HEMLINE RIBBING

Ch 9

Row 1: Sl st in second ch from hook and in each ch across, turn. (8 sts)

Row 2: Ch 1; working in back loops only, sl st in each st across, turn.

Repeat Row 2 until you have completed a total of 166 [182, 202, 218, 234, 254] rows or until ribbing is long enough to go around entire bottom edge of cardigan.

Fasten off, leaving a long tail for sewing. Using a tapestry needle and tail, sew the ribbing to bottom edge of cardigan.

COLLAR

Ch 8

Row 1: Sl st in second ch from hook and in each ch across, turn. (7 sc)

Row 2: Ch 1; working in back loops only, sl st in each st across, turn.

Repeat Row 2 for a total of 190 [190, 194, 194, 194, 198] rows or until ribbing is long enough to reach around the entire inner edge of cardigan.

Fasten off, leaving a long tail for sewing. Using tapestry needle and tail, sew the collar around the entire inner edge of cardigan.

Weave in ends.

CASHEL
CARDIGAN

This long, oversized cardigan features a textured stitch reminiscent of the knit waffle stitch, providing a cozy and stylish layer for any outfit. Its relaxed fit and generous length ensure comfort and warmth, making it perfect for chilly days. Ideal for casual outings, it adds a chic touch to any wardrobe.

SKILL LEVEL
Easy

LIST OF MATERIALS
Hobbii, Winter Glow Solid – Amber
(7 oz, 766 yds / 200 g, 700 m);
4 [5, 5, 6, 6, 7] balls

Size H-8 (5 mm) hook

Tapestry Needle

GAUGE
17 sts = 4" (10 cm); 12 rows = 4" (10 cm)

ABBREVIATIONS
ch: chain
hdc: half double crochet
st(s): stitch(es)

SIZING

Instructions given for Small, with changes for Medium, Large, XL, 2XL, 3XL are in [ ].

SIZE	S	M	L	XL	2XL	3XL
Finished Bust	44" 118 cm	48" 122 cm	52" 132 cm	56" 142 cm	60" 152 cm	64" 162 cm
Shoulder to Shoulder	22" 56 cm	24" 61 cm	26" 66 cm	28" 71 cm	30" 76 cm	32" 81 cm
Length	28" 71 cm	28" 71 cm	28" 71 cm	28" 71 cm	28" 71 cm	28" 71 cm
Sleeve Length	18" 46 cm	18" 46 cm	18" 46 cm	18" 46 cm	18" 46 cm	18" 46 cm

Pattern Notes

Ch 1 at beginning of row does NOT count as first stitch

BACK PANEL

Ch 127 (All sizes)

Row 1: Hdc in second ch from hook and in each ch across, turn. (126 hdc)

Row 2: Ch 1; *working in **back loops** only, hdc; working in **front loops** only, hdc; repeat from * across until 8 sts remain; working in the **back loops** only, hdc 8, turn.

Row 3: Ch 1; working in the **back loops** only, hdc 8; *working in **front loops** only, hdc; working in **back loops** only, hdc; repeat from * across, turn.

Rows 4-67 [73, 79, 85, 91, 97]: (64 [70, 76, 82, 88, 94] rows) Repeat Rows 2-3.

Fasten off and weave in ends.

FRONT PANELS (Make 2)

Ch 127 (All sizes)

Rows 1-3: (3 rows) Repeat Rows 1-3 of Back Panel.

Rows 4-25 [29, 31, 35, 37, 41]: (22 [26, 28, 32, 34, 38] rows) Repeat Rows 2-3 of Back Panel.

Fasten off, leaving a long tail for seaming.

SLEEVES (Make 2)

Ch 77 (All sizes)

Rows 1-3: (3 rows) Repeat Rows 1-3 of Back Panel.

Rows 4-43 [45, 47, 49, 53, 55]: (40 [42, 44, 46, 50, 52] rows) Repeat Rows 2-3 of Back Panel.

Fasten off, leaving a long tail for seaming. Fold fabric in half lengthwise, so the edges line up. Using tapestry needle and tail, seam the edges together.

ASSEMBLY

Joining Panels

Lay front panels on back panels, lining up edges of row ends. Using tapestry needle and tail, seam both layers together using a whip stitch.

Joining Sleeves

Align sleeves with armhole of body of cardigan. Using a tapestry needle and tail, seam through both layers to join. Leave remaining tail to seam sides.

Seaming Sides

Using tapestry needle and remaining tail, seam the sides of front and back panels together.

COLLAR

Ch 10

Row 1: Hdc in second ch from the hook and in each ch across, turn. [9 hdc]

Row 2: Ch 1; working in **back loops** only, hdc in each st across, turn.

Repeat Row 2 for a total of 271 [269, 271, 269, 271, 269] times or until ribbing is long enough to reach around the entire cardigan.

Fasten off, leaving a long tail for sewing. Using tapestry needle and tail, sew the collar around the entire inner edge of cardigan.

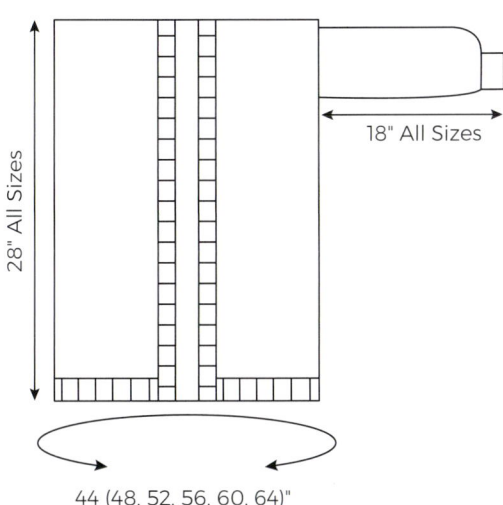

28" All Sizes

18" All Sizes

44 (48, 52, 56, 60, 64)"

CLEGGAN CREW
NECK SWEATER

This textured crew neck sweater showcases some basic crochet stitches that create a rich, dimensional fabric, providing warmth and style. The classic crew neck design offers a timeless silhouette, making it perfect for layering or casual wear.

SKILL LEVEL
Easy

LIST OF MATERIALS
Drops Merino, Extra Fine – Off White
(1 ¾ oz, 115 yds / 50 g, 105 m);
12 [13, 13, 14, 14, 15] balls

Size I-9 (5.5 mm) hook

Size 7 (4.5 mm) hook

Stitch Marker

Tapestry Needle

GAUGE
21 sts = 4" (10 cm); 19 rows = 4" (10 cm)

ABBREVIATIONS
ch: chain
ch-1 sp: chain 1 space
sc: single crochet
sc2tog: single crochet 2 together
sl st: slip stitch
st(s): stitch(es)

SIZING

Instructions given for Small, with changes for Medium, Large, XL, 2XL, 3XL are in [ ].

SIZE	S	M	L	XL	2XL	3XL
Finished Bust	44" 112 cm	48" 122 cm	51" 129.5 cm	55" 140 cm	59" 150 cm	63" 160 cm
Shoulder to Shoulder	22" 56 cm	24" 61 cm	25½" 65 cm	27½ " 70 cm	29½ " 75 cm	31½ " 80 cm
Length	20" 51 cm	20" 51 cm	20½" 52 cm	21" 53 cm	23" 58.5 cm	23" 58.5 cm

Special Stitches

Single Crochet 2 Together (sc2tog):
[Insert hook in next st or sp indicated and pull up a loop] twice, *(three lps on hook)*, yo, draw through all loops on hook.

Pattern Notes

Ch 1 at beginning of row does NOT count as first stitch

BACK PANEL

With Size I-9 (5.5 mm) hook

Ch 116 [126, 134, 144, 154, 164]

Row 1: Sc in second ch from hook, *ch 1, skip next ch, sc in next ch; repeat from * across, turn. (115 [125, 133, 143, 153, 163] sts)

Row 2: Ch 1, sc in first st, ch 1, skip next ch-1 sp, *sc in next st, ch 1, skip next ch-1 sp; repeat from * across, sc in last st, turn.

Repeat Row 2 until you have completed a total of 94 [94, 96, 98, 108, 108] rows.

Fasten off.

FRONT PANEL

With Size I-9 (5.5 mm) hook

Ch 116 [126, 134, 144, 154, 164]

Rows 1-2: *(2 rows)* Repeat Rows 1-2 of Back Panel. (115 [125, 133, 143, 153, 163] sts)

Repeat Row 2 until you have completed a total of 82 [82, 84, 86, 96, 96] rows.

SHAPE LEFT NECK

Row 1: *(Right Side)* Ch 1, sc in first st, [ch 1, skip next ch-1 sp, sc in next st] repeat 23 [25, 27, 29, 31 34] times, sc2tog, turn. (48 [52, 56, 60, 64, 70] sts)

Row 2: Ch 1, sc2tog, [ch 1, skip next st, sc in next st; repeat from * across, turn. (47 [51, 55, 59, 63, 69] sts)

Row 3: Ch 1, sc in first st, *ch 1, skip next st, sc in next st; repeat from * across until 2 sts remain, sc2tog, turn. (46 [50, 54, 58, 62, 68] sts)

Rows 4-11: *(8 rows)* Repeat Rows 2-3, decreasing one st each row.

Row 12: Repeat Row 2. (37 [41, 45, 49, 53, 59] sts)

Fasten off, leaving a long tail.

SHAPE RIGHT NECK

With the right side facing, count 49 [53, 57, 61, 65, 71] sts from last st of Row 82 [82, 84, 86, 96, 96] and rejoin yarn.

Row 1: Ch 1, sc2tog, sc, *ch 1, skip next st, sc in next st; repeat from * across, turn. (48 [52, 56, 60, 64, 70] sts)

Row 2: Ch 1, sc in first st, ch 1, skip next st *sc in next st, ch 1, skip next st; repeat from * across until 2 sts remain, sc2tog, turn. (47 [51, 55, 59, 63, 69] sts)

Row 3: Ch 1, sc2tog, sc in next st, *ch 1, skip next st, sc; repeat from * across, turn. (46 [50, 54, 58, 62, 68] sts)

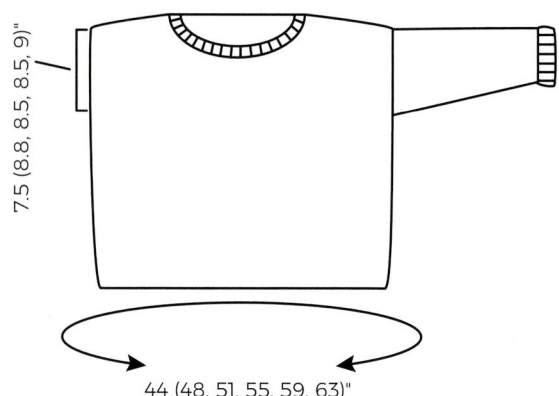

7.5 (8.8, 8.5, 8.5, 9)"

44 (48, 51, 55, 59, 63)"

Rows 4-11: *(8 rows)* Repeat Rows 2-3, decreasing one st each row.

Row 12: Repeat Row 2. (37 [41, 45, 49, 53, 59] sts)

Fasten off, leaving a long tail.

SLEEVES (Make 2)

Cuff

With Size 7 (4.5 mm) hook

Ch 9

Row 1: Sc in second ch from hook and in each ch across, turn. (8 sc)

Row 2: Ch 1; working in **back loops** only, sc in each st across, turn.

Repeat Row 2 until you have completed a total of 39 [43, 43, 47, 47, 51] rows.

Turn to work into row ends.

Body

With Size I-9 (5.5 mm) hook

Row 1: Ch 1, sc in first row end, *ch 1, skip next row end, sc in next row end; repeat from * across, turn. (39 [43, 43, 47, 47, 51] sts)

Rows 2-3: Ch 1, sc in first st, *ch 1, skip next st, sc in next st; repeat from * across, turn.

Row 4: Ch 1, 2 sc in first st, ch 1, skip next st,*sc in next st, ch 1, skip next st; repeat from * across until one st remains, 2 sc in last st, turn. (41 [45, 45, 49, 49, 53] sts)

Row 5: Ch 1, sc in each of next 2 sts, ch 1, skip next st, *sc in next st, ch 1, skip next st; repeat from * across until 2 sts remain, sc in each of next 2 sts, turn. (41 [45, 45, 49, 49, 53] sts)

Rows 6-8: *(3 rows)* Repeat Row 5. (41 [45, 45, 49, 49, 53] sts)

Row 9: Ch 1, sc in first st, ch 1, *sc in next st, ch 1, skip next st; repeat from * across until 2 sts remain, sc in next st, ch 1, sc in last st, turn. (43 [47, 47, 51, 51, 55] sts)

Rows 10-12: *(3 rows)* Ch, sc in first st, *ch 1, skip next st, sc in next st; repeat from * across, turn (43 [47, 47, 51, 51, 55] sts)

Repeat Rows 4-12 seven more times.

Row 76: Ch 1, sc in first st, *ch 1, skip next st, sc in next st; repeat from * across, turn. (77 [81, 81, 85, 85, 89] sts)

Fasten off, leaving a long tail for seaming. Fold fabric in half lengthwise, so the edges line up. Using tapestry needle and tail, seam the edges together.

ASSEMBLY

Joining Panels

Lay front panels on back panels, lining up edges of row ends. Using tapestry needle and tail, seam through both layers at the shoulder seam using a whip stitch.

Seaming Sides

Using tapestry needle and tail, seam the sides of front and back panels together, leaving a 7½ [8, 8, 8½, 9, 9]" / 19 [20, 20, 21.5, 23, 23] cm opening for sleeves.

Joining Sleeves

Align sleeves with armhole of body. Using a tapestry needle and tail, seam through both layers to join. Weave in ends.

COLLAR

With front panels facing, rejoin yarn to one shoulder seam.

Set-Up Round: Ch 1, sc in each st around neckline, sl st in first sc to join.

Ch 6

Row 1: Sc in second ch from hook and in each ch across, sl st in each of next 2 sts from Set-Up round, turn. [5 sc]

Row 2: Do not ch; skip first 2 sl sts; working in **back loops** only, sc in each of next 4 sts; sc in last st, turn.

Row 3: Ch 1, sc in first st; working in **back loops** only, sc in each of next 4 sts; sl st in next 2 sts from Set-Up Round, turn.

Repeat Rows 2-3 until you have created the ribbing around the entire Set-Up Round. Fasten off, leaving a long tail. Using tapestry needle and tail, seam first and last rows of ribbing together. Weave in ends.

CONNEMARA POCKET SHAWL

This easy pocket shawl offers both style and practicality, providing warmth like a traditional shawl while featuring pockets for added convenience. It's perfect for chilly days and would even make a thoughtful gift to someone special.

SKILL LEVEL

Easy

LIST OF MATERIALS

Lion Brand, Wool-Ease – Fisherman
(3 oz, 197 yds / 85 g, 180 m); 6 balls

Size I-9 (5.5 mm) hook

Tapestry Needle

GAUGE

14 sts = 4" (10 cm); 11 rows = 4" (10 cm)

ABBREVIATIONS

ch: chain
dc: double crochet
sc: single crochet
st(s): stitch(es)

MEASUREMENTS

65" (165 cm) Long / 16" (40 cm) Wide without fringe

Pattern Notes

Ch 1 at beginning of row does NOT count as the first stitch.

Ch 2 at the beginning of a row does NOT count as the first stitch.

NECKLINE RIBBING

Ch 9

Row 1: Sc in second ch from hook and in each ch across, turn (8 sc)

Row 2: Ch 1, sc in first st; working in **back loops** only. sc in each of next 6 sts, sc in last st, turn.

Rows 3- 228: Repeat Row 2.

Turn to work into row ends.

MAIN SECTION

Row 1: Ch 1, sc in each row end, turn. (228 sc)

Row 2: (Right Side) Ch 2, dc in same st as ch 2, dc in each of next 3 sts, *skip next st, dc in each of next 3 sts, dc in previous skipped st, dc in each of next 4 sts; repeat from * across, turn.

Row 3: Ch 1, sc in each st across, turn.

Rows 4-39: (36 rows) Repeat Rows 2-3.

Fasten off and weave in ends.

POCKETS (Make 2)

Ch 37

Row 1: Sc in second ch from hook and in each ch across, turn. (36 sc)

Row 2: (Right Side) Ch 2, dc in same st as ch 2, dc in each of next 3 sts, *skip next st, dc in each of next 3 sts, dc in previous skipped st, dc in each of next 4 sts; repeat from * across, turn.

Row 3: Ch 1, sc in each st across, turn.

Rows 4-13: (10 rows) Repeat Rows 2-3.

Fasten off, leaving a long tail for sewing.

ASSEMBLY

With right side facing, lay shawl length wise. Center wrong side of each pocket onto shawl approximately 1" (3 cm) from short end of shawl.

Using tapestry needle and tail, sew the sides and bottom of each pocket onto shawl, leaving an opening at the top.

Fasten off and weave in ends.

Fringe

Cut multiple 24" (61 cm) strands of yarn. Fold 3-4 strands of yarn in half to create a loop, insert hook into first stitch of short side of shawl, pull loop of yarn strands through stitch, pull tails ends through loop to secure. Continue to evenly add fringe across short end. Repeat for opposite side. Trim fringe to desired length.

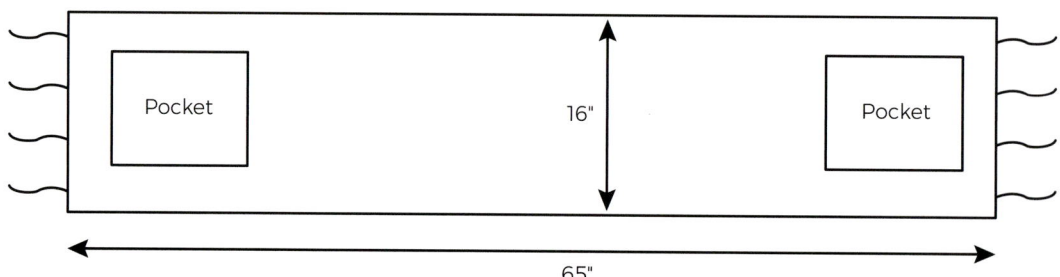

ELLY
BOBBLE CARDIGAN

This stunning cardigan adds texture and warmth with its raised, plush bobble design. Cozy and fashionable this cardigan is perfect for layering, offering a unique and playful touch to any wardrobe.

SKILL LEVEL
Intermediate

LIST OF MATERIALS
Lion Brand, Touch of Alpaca – Golden Rod
(3 ½ oz, 207 yds / 100 g, 190 m);
8 [8, 9, 9, 10, 10] balls

Size I-9 (5.5 mm) hook

Tapestry Needle

GAUGE
15 sts = 4" (10 cm); 12 rows = 4" (10 cm)

ABBREVIATIONS
bo: bobble
ch: chain
hdc: half double crochet
sc: single crochet
sl st: slip stitch
st(s): stitch(es)

SIZING

Instructions given for Small, with changes for Medium, Large, XL, 2XL, 3XL are in [ ].

SIZE	S	M	L	XL	2XL	3XL
Finished Bust	42" 107 cm	46" 117 cm	50" 127 cm	54" 137 cm	58" 147 cm	62" 157.5 cm
Shoulder to Shoulder	21" 53 cm	23" 58.5 cm	25" 63.5 cm	27" 68.5 cm	29" 74 cm	31" 79 cm
Length	25" 63.5 cm	25" 63.5 cm	25" 63.5 cm	27" 68.5 cm	27" 68.5 cm	27" 68.5 cm

Pattern Notes

Ch 1 at beginning of row does NOT count as first stitch.

BACK PANEL

Ch 90 [90, 90, 99, 99, 99]

Row 1: *(Right Side)* Hdc in second ch from hook and in each of ch across until 8 ch remain, sc in each of the next 8 ch, turn. (89 [89, 89, 98, 98, 98] sts)

Row 2: Ch 1; working in **back loops** only, sc in each of next 8 sts; working in **back loops** only, hdc in each of next 4 sts; bo in next st, *working in **back loops** only, hdc in each of next 8 sts; bo in next st; repeat from * across until 4 sts remain; working in the **back loops** only, hdc in each of next 4 sts, turn.

Row 3: Ch 1; working in the **back loops** only, hdc in each st across until 8 sts remain; working in the **back loops** only, sc in each of next 8 sts, turn.

Row 4: Ch 1; working in **back loops** only, sc in each of the next 8 sts; working in **back loops** only, hdc in each st across, turn.

Row 5: Repeat Row 3.

Row 6: Ch 1; working in **back loops** only, sc in each of next 8 sts; *working in **back loops** only, hdc in each of next 8 sts; bo in next st; repeat from * across until 9 sts remain; working in the **back loops** only, hdc in each of next 9 sts, turn.

Row 7: Repeat Row 3.

Row 8: Repeat Row 4.

Row 9: Repeat Row 3.

Repeat Rows 2-9 until you have completed a total of 63 [67, 75, 79, 87, 91] rows. Fasten off. Weave in ends.

FRONT PANEL (Make 2)

Ch 90 [90, 90, 99, 99, 99]

Rows 1-9: *(9 rows)* Repeat Rows 1-9 of Back Panel.

Repeat Rows 2-9 until you have completed a total of 23 [27, 31, 35, 39, 39] rows. Fasten off, leaving a long tail for seaming.

SLEEVES (Make 2)

Ch 63 (All sizes)

Row 1: Hdc in second ch from hook and in each of ch across until 8 ch remain, sl st in each of the next 8 ch, turn. (62 sts)

Row 2: Ch 1; working in **back loops** only, sl st in each of next 8 sts; working in **back loops** only, hdc in each of next 4 sts; bo in next st, *working in **back loops** only, hdc in each of next 8 sts; bo in next st; repeat from * across until 4 sts remain; working in the **back loops** only, hdc in each of next 4 sts, turn.

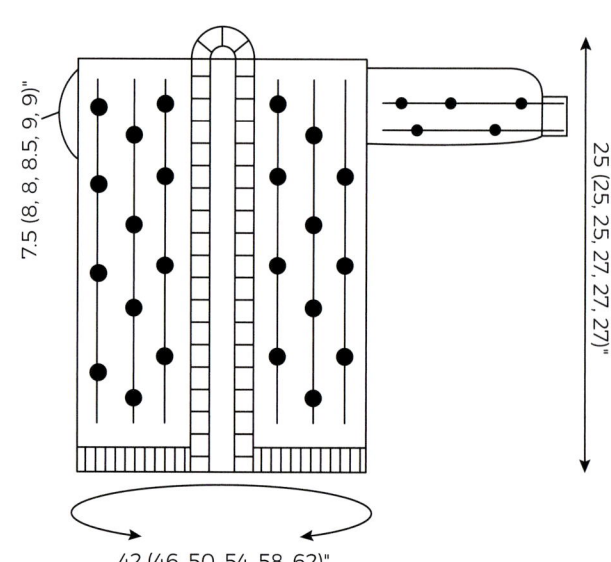

Row 3: Ch 1; working in the **back loops** only, hdc in each st across until 8 sts remain; working in the **back loops** only, sl st in each of next 8 sts, turn.

Row 4: Ch 1; working in **back loops** only, sl st in each of the next 8 sts; working in **back loops** only, hdc in each st across, turn.

Row 5: Repeat Row 3.

Row 6: Ch 1; working in **back loops** only, sl st in each of next 8 sts; *working in **back loops** only, hdc in each of next 8 sts; bo in next st; repeat from * across until 9 sts remain; working in the **back loops** only, hdc in each of next 9 sts, turn.

Row 7: Repeat Row 3.

Row 8: Repeat Row 4.

Row 9: Repeat Row 3.

Repeat Rows 2-9 until you have completed a total of 44 [48, 48, 52, 56, 56] rows.

Fasten off, leaving a long tail for seaming. Fold fabric in half lengthwise, so the edges line up. Using tapestry needle and tail, seam the edges together.

ASSEMBLY

Joining Panels

With right sides touching, lay the front panels on back panel, lining row ends at shoulder seam. Using tapestry needle and tail, seam the shoulders together using a whip stitch.

Seaming Sides

Using tapestry needle and tail, seam the sides of front and back panels together, leaving a 7½ [8, 8, 8½, 9, 9]" / 19 [20, 20, 21.5, 23, 23] cm opening for sleeves.

Joining Sleeves

Align sleeves with armhole of body. Using a tapestry needle and tail, seam through both layers to join. Weave in ends.

COLLAR

With front panels facing, rejoin yarn to bottom right front panel.

Set-up Row: Ch 1, sc evenly into each st of right panel, sc evenly across back, sc evenly into each st of left panel.

Ch 9

Row 1: Sc in second ch from hook and in each ch across, sl st in each of next 2 sts from Set-Up Row, turn. (8 sc)

Row 2: Do NOT ch; skip first 2 sl sts; working in **back loops** only, sc in each of next 7 sts; sc in last st, turn.

Row 3: Ch 1, sc in first st; working in **back loops** only, sc in each of next 7sts; sl st in next 2 sts from Set-Up Row, turn.

Repeat Rows 2-3 until you have created the ribbing around the entire Set-Up Row. Fasten off. Weave in ends.

FANORE
SWEATER SCARF

This innovative crochet scarf with sleeves doubles as a wrap-around sweater, combining style and functionality. Crafted with a textured stitch that mimics knitting, it offers warmth and comfort without feeling weighed down. Perfect for layering, this versatile accessory adds a cozy touch to any outfit, making it a must-have for chilly days.

SKILL LEVEL

Intermediate

LIST OF MATERIALS

Lion Brand, Touch of Alpaca – Golden Rod
(3 ½ oz, 207 yds / 100 g, 190 m);
8 [8, 9, 9, 10, 10] balls

Size I-9 (5.5 mm) hook

Tapestry Needle

GAUGE

15 sts = 4" (10 cm); 12 rows = 4" (10 cm)

ABBREVIATIONS

ch: chain
hdc: half double crochet
sc: single crochet
sl st: slip stitch
st(s): stitch(es)

SIZING

Instructions given for Small/Medium, with changes for Large/Xtra Large and 2XL/3XL are in [ ].

SIZE	S/M	L/XL	2XL/3XL
To Fit Bust Size	32-38" 81-96.5 cm	40-46" 102-117 cm	48-54" 122-137 cm
Length Without Cuff	78" 198 cm	88" 223.5 cm	102" 259 cm
Cuff Length	10" 25.5cm	10" 25.5 cm	10" 25.5 cm
Width	16" 41 cm	18" 46 cm	20" 51 cm

Pattern Notes

Ch 1 at beginning of row does NOT count as the first stitch.

Ch 2 at the beginning of a row does NOT count as the first stitch.

FANORE SWEATER SCARF

Leaving a long tail, Ch 491 [541, 611]

Row 1: Sl st in second ch from hook, sl st in each of next 49 ch; *hdc in next st, sl st in next; repeat from * across until 50 ch remain, sl st in each of next 50 sts, turn. (490 [540, 610] sts)

Row 2: Ch 1; working in **back loops** only, sl st in each of next 50 sts; *working in **back loops** only, sl st in next st; working in **back loops** only, hdc in the next st; repeat from * across until 50 sts remain; working in **back loops** only, sl st in each of next 50 sts, turn.

Row 3: *(Wrong Side)* Ch 1; working in **back loops** only, sl st in each of next 50 sts; *working in **back loops** only, hdc in next st; working in **back loops** only, sl st in the next st; repeat from * across until 50 sts remain; working in **back loops** only, sl st in each of next 50 sts, turn.

Repeat Rows 2-3 until the main body measures 16 [18, 20]" / 41 [46, 51] cm wide.

Fasten off, leaving a long tail.

SEAMING SLEEVES

With wrong side facing, fold fabric in half lengthwise, so the edges of cuffs line up. Using tapestry needle and tail, seam the edges of cuffs together. Weave in ends.

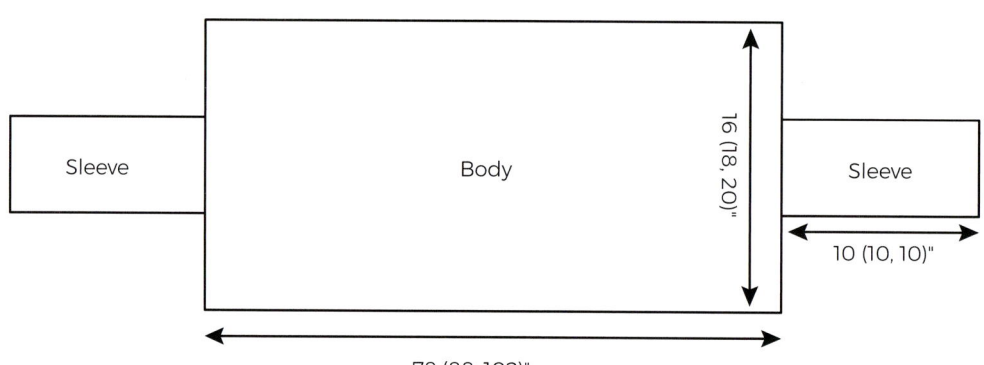

FAWNMORE
RIBBED CARDIGAN

This long, ribbed, and oversized cardigan features a wide ribbed collar that adds a cozy, stylish touch. The relaxed fit provides comfort and versatility, making it ideal for layering over various outfits. Perfect for chilly days, this cardigan combines warmth with modern elegance, elevating any casual look effortlessly.

SKILL LEVEL
Easy

LIST OF MATERIALS

Sirdar, Hayfield Bonus Aran with Wool – Green Heather
(14 oz, 912 yds / 400 g, 840 m);

2 [2, 3, 3, 4, 4] balls

Size K-10 ½ (6.5 mm) hook

Tapestry Needle

GAUGE
12 sts = 4" (10 cm); 9 rows = 4" (10 cm)

ABBREVIATIONS
ch: chain
hdc: half double crochet
sc: single crochet
sl st: slip stitch
st(s): stitch(es)

SIZING

Instructions given for Small, with changes for Medium, Large, XL, 2XL, 3XL are in [ ].

SIZE	S	M	L	XL	2XL	3XL
Finished Bust	42" 107 cm	45" 114 cm	47" 119 cm	50" 127 cm	55" 140 cm	58" 147 cm
Shoulder to Shoulder	21" 53 cm	22 ½" 57 cm	23 ½" 60 cm	25" 63.5 cm	27 ½" 70 cm	29" 74 cm
Length	28" 63.5 cm	28" 63.5 cm	28" 63.5 cm	28" 63.5 cm	28" 63.5 cm	28" 63.5 cm

FIRST FRONT PANEL

Ch 85 (for all sizes)

Row 1: Hdc in second ch from hook and in each ch across, turn. (84 hdc)

Row 2: Ch 1; working in **back loops** only, hdc in each st across, turn.

Rows 3-16 [18, 20, 22, 24, 26]: Repeat Row 2.

Do NOT fasten off. Continue to Back Panel.

BACK PANEL

Row 1: Ch 1; working in **back loops** only, hdc in each of next 62 [60, 60, 58, 58, 56] sts, leave remaining sts unworked, turn.

Row 2: Ch 23 [25, 25, 27, 27, 29], hdc in second ch from hook and in each of next 21 [23, 23, 25, 25, 27] chains; working in **back loops** only, hdc in each of next 62 [60, 60, 58, 58, 56] sts, turn.

Row 3: Ch 1; working in **back loops** only, hdc in each st across, turn.

Rows 4-48 [50, 52, 56, 62, 66]: *(45 [47, 49, 53, 59, 63] rows)* Repeat Row 3.

Do NOT fasten off. Continue to Second Front Panel.

SECOND FRONT PANEL

Rows 1-3: *(3 rows)* Repeat Rows 1-3 of Back Panel.

Rows 4-16 [18, 20, 22, 24, 26]: *(13 [15, 17, 19, 21, 23] rows)* Repeat Row 3 of Back Panel.

Fasten off.

SLEEVES (Make 2)

Ch 56 (All sizes)

Row 1: Hdc in second ch from hook, hdc in each of next 47 ch, sl st in each of next 7 ch, turn (55 sts)

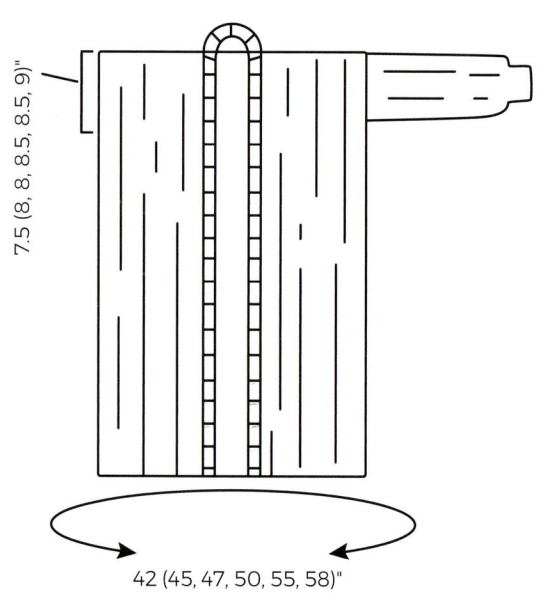

7.5 (8, 8, 8.5, 8.5, 9)"

42 (45, 47, 50, 55, 58)"

Row 2: Ch 1; working in **back loops** only sl st in each of next 7 sts; working in **back loops** only, hdc in each of next 48 sts, turn.

Row 3: Ch 1; working in **back loops** only hdc in each of next 48 sts; working in **back loops** only, sl st in each of next 7 sts, turn.

Rows 4-35 [37, 37, 39, 39, 41]: *(32 [34, 34, 36, 36, 38] rows)* Repeat Rows 2-3.

Fasten off, leaving a long tail for seaming. Fold fabric in half lengthwise, so the edges line up. Using tapestry needle and tail, seam the edges together.

ASSEMBLY

Joining Panels

Lay the front panels on back panel, lining row ends at shoulder seam. Using tapestry needle and tail, seam the shoulders together using a whip stitch, making sure to seam across to armholes.

Joining Sleeves

Align sleeves with armhole of body. Using a tapestry needle and tail, seam through both layers to join. Weave in ends.

COLLAR

With front panels facing, rejoin yarn to bottom right front panel

Set-Up Row: Ch 1, sc evenly into each st of right panel, sc evenly across back, sc evenly into each st of left panel.

Ch 13

Row 1: Sc in second ch from hook and in each ch across, sl st in each of next 2 sts from Set-Up Row, turn. (12 sc)

Row 2: Do NOT ch; skip first 2 sl sts; working in **back loops** only, sc in each of next 12 sts, turn.

Row 3: Ch 1; working in **back loops** only, sc in each of next 12 sts; sl st in next 2 sts from Set-Up Row, turn.

Repeat Rows 2-3 until you have created the ribbing around the entire Set-Up Row. Fasten off. Weave in ends.

FOXFORD
V NECK SWEATER

A crochet V-neck sweater offers a stylish and versatile wardrobe staple, featuring a flattering neckline and comfortable fit. Perfect for layering or wearing on its own.

SKILL LEVEL
Intermediate

LIST OF MATERIALS
Drops, Karisma – Light Beige Brown
(1.8 oz, 109 yds / 50 g, 100 m);
13 [14, 14, 15, 15, 16] balls

Size H-8 (5 mm) hook

Tapestry Needle

GAUGE
15 sts = 4" (10 cm); 11 rows = 4" (10 cm)

ABBREVIATIONS
BPdc: back post double crochet
ch: chain
FPdc: front post double crochet
hdc2tog: half double crochet 2 together
hdc: half double crochet
sc: single crochet
sl st: slip stitch
st(s): stitch(es)

SIZING

Instructions given for Small, with changes for Medium, Large, XL, 2XL, 3XL are in [ ].

SIZE	S	M	L	XL	2XL	3XL
Finished Bust	44" 118 cm	48" 122 cm	52" 132 cm	56" 142 cm	60" 152 cm	64" 162 cm
Shoulder to Shoulder	22" 56 cm	24" 61 cm	26" 66 cm	28" 71 cm	30" 76 cm	32" 81 cm
Length	22" 56 cm	23" 59 cm	24" 61 cm	24" 61 cm	25" 63 cm	25" 63 cm
Sleeve Length	18" 46 cm	18" 46 cm	18" 46 cm	18" 46 cm	18" 46 cm	18" 46 cm

Special Stitches

Half Double Crochet 2 Together (hdc2tog):
[yo, insert hook into next st indicated, pull up a loop] twice, *(5 loops on hook)*, yo, draw through all loops on hook.

Pattern Notes

Ch 1 at beginning of row does NOT count as first stitch
Ch 3 at beginning of row does NOT count as first stitch

BACK PANEL

Ribbed Hem

Ch 10 (All sizes)

Row 1: Sc in second ch from the hook and in each ch across, turn (9 sc)

Row 2: Ch 1; working in **back loops** only, sc in each st across, turn.

Repeat Row 2 until you have a total of 82 [90, 98, 104, 112, 120] rows.

Turn to work into row ends.

Body

Row 1: Ch 1, hdc in each row end, turn. (82 [90, 98, 104, 112, 120] hdc)

Row 2: Ch 1, hdc in each st across, turn.

Repeat Row 2 until you have a total of 60 [62, 66, 66, 68, 68] rows.

Fasten off.

FRONT PANEL

Ribbed Hem

Repeat as for Ribbed Hem of Back Panel.

Turn to work into row ends.

Body

Rows 1-2: *(2 rows)* Repeat Row 1 and 2 for Body of Back Panel.

Repeat Row 2 until you have completed a total of 38 [40, 44, 44, 46, 46] rows.

V-NECK

Side 1

Row 1: *(Right Side)* Ch 1, hdc in each of next 39 [43, 47, 50, 54, 58] sts, hdc2tog, turn. (40 [44, 48, 51, 55, 59] hdc)

Place marker in next st. This is where you will begin Side 2.

Row 2: Ch 1, hdc2tog, hdc in each st across, turn. (39 [43, 47, 50, 54, 58] hdc)

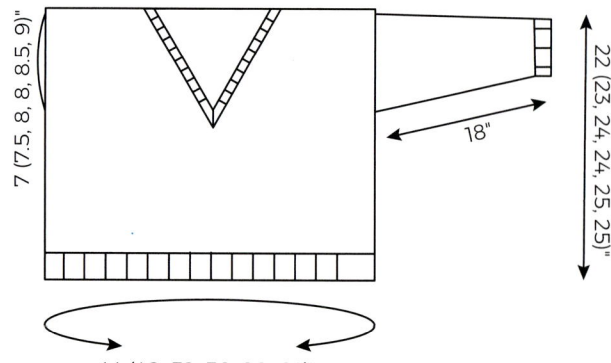

Row 3: Ch 1, hdc in each st across until 2 sts remain, hdc2tog, turn. (38 [42, 46, 49, 53, 57] hdc)

Row 4: Ch 1, hdc2tog, hdc in each st across, turn. (37 [41, 45, 48, 52, 56] hdc)

Rows 5-22: *(18 rows)* Repeat Rows 3 and 4. (19 [23, 27, 30, 34, 38] hdc)

Fasten off, leaving a long tail for seaming.

Side 2

With right side facing, rejoin yarn to marked st.

Row 1: Ch 1, hdc2tog, hdc in each st across, turn. (40 [44, 48, 51, 55, 59] hdc)

Row 2: Ch 1, hdc in each st across until 2 sts remain, hdc2tog, turn. (39 [43, 47, 50, 54, 58] hdc)

Rows 3-22: *(20 rows)* Repeat Rows 1 and 2. (19 [23, 27, 30, 34, 38] hdc)

Fasten off, leaving a long tail for seaming

SLEEVES (Make 2)

Cuff

Ch 10

Row 1: Sc in second ch from hook and in each ch across, turn. (9 sc)

Row 2: Ch 1; working in **back loops** only, sc in each st across, turn.

Repeat Row 2 until you have a total of 36 [38, 38, 40, 42, 42] rows.

Turn to work into row ends.

Sleeve body

Row 1: Ch 1, hdc in each row end, turn. (36 [38, 38, 40, 42, 42] hdc)

For the remainder of the sleeve, work as follows for specified size below:

When instructed to increase, work the row as follows: Ch 1, 2 hdc in first st, hdc across until 1 st remains, 2 hdc in last st, turn.

Work all non-increase rows as follows: Ch 1, hdc in each st across, turn.

Work a total of 48 rows for all sizes while increasing in the following rows:

S: 6, 12, 18, 24, 30, 36, 42, 48. (52 hdc)

M: 6, 12, 18, 24, 30, 36, 42, 48. (54 hdc)

L: 4, 8, 12, 16, 20, 24, 28, 32, 36, 40, 44. (60 hdc)

XL: 4, 8, 12, 16, 20, 24, 28, 32, 36, 40. (60 hdc)

2XL: 4, 8, 12, 16, 20, 24, 28, 32, 36, 40, 44. (64 hdc)

3XL: 4, 8, 12, 16, 20, 24, 28, 32, 36, 40, 44, 48. (68 hdc)

Fasten off, leaving a long tail for seaming. Fold fabric in half lengthwise, so the edges line up. Using tapestry needle and tail, seam the edges together.

ASSEMBLY

Joining Panels

Lay front panel on back panel, lining up edges of row ends. Using tapestry needle and tail, seam each side of front panel through both layers using a whip stitch.

Seaming Sides

Using tapestry needle and tail, seam the sides of front and back panels together leaving a 7 [7 ½ , 8, 8, 8 ½, 9]" (18 [19, 20, 20, 21.5, 23] cm) opening for sleeves.

Joining Sleeves

Align sleeves with armhole of body. Using a tapestry needle and tail, seam through both layers to join. Weave in ends.

NECKLINE FINISHING

With front panels facing, rejoin yarn to the neckline at the left shoulder seam.

Set-Up Round: Ch 1, sc evenly into each row end of left panel, sc evenly into each row end of right panel, sc evenly across back, sl st to first sc to join. (st count should be an even number)

Round 1: Ch 3, dc in each st around, sl st to beginning ch 3 to join.

Rounds 2-3: *(2 rounds)* Ch 3, *FPdc in next st, BPdc in the next; repeat from * around, sl st to beginning ch 3 to join.

Fasten off and weave in all remaining ends.

KINGSTOWN
SWEATER VEST

This round neck vest top features the textured lemon peel stitch, combining simple single and double crochets for a subtle, pebble like effect. Lightweight and breathable, it's perfect for layering or wearing on its own in warmer weather. The versatile design adds a stylish, handmade touch to any outfit.

SKILL LEVEL
Intermediate

LIST OF MATERIALS
Sesia, Nordica
100% Superwash Wool – Rust
(1 ¾ oz, 137 yds / 50 g, 125 m);
7 [8, 8, 9, 10, 10] balls

Size J-10 (6 mm) hook

Tapestry Needle

GAUGE
14 sts = 4" (10 cm); 15 rows = 4" (10 cm)

ABBREVIATIONS
ch: chain
dc: double crochet
sc: single crochet
sc2tog: single crochet 2 together
sl st: slip stitch
st(s): stitch(es)

SIZING

Instructions given for Small, with changes for Medium, Large, XL, 2XL, 3XL are in [ ].

SIZE	S	M	L	XL	2XL	3XL
Finished Bust	38" 96.5 cm	41" 104 cm	42 ½" 108 cm	46" 117 cm	50" 127 cm	53 ½" 136 cm
Total Length	20" 51 cm	21" 53 cm	22" 56 cm	23" 58.5 cm	24" 61 cm	24" 61 cm

Special Stitches

Single Crochet 2 Together (sc2tog):
[Insert hook in next st or sp indicated and pull up a loop] twice, *(three lps on hook)*, yo, draw through all loops on hook.

Pattern Notes

Ch 1 at beginning of row does NOT count as first stitch
Ch 3 at beginning of row counts as first stitch.

BACK PANEL

Bottom Ribbing

Ch 9

Row 1: Sc in second ch from hook and in each ch across, turn. (8 sc)

Row 2: Ch 1; working in **back loops** only, sc in each st across, turn.

Repeat Row 2 until you have completed a total of 67 [71, 75, 81, 87, 93] rows.

Turn to work into row ends.

Body

Row 1: Ch 1, single crochet into each of next 67 [71, 75, 81, 87, 93] row ends, turn. (67 [71, 75, 81, 87, 93] sts)

Row 2: Ch 1, sc in first st, *dc in next st, sc in next; repeat from * across, turn.

Row 3: Ch 3, *sc in next st, dc in next st; repeat from * across, turn.

Repeat Rows 2-3 until you have completed a total of 33 [35, 37, 39, 41, 43] rows.

Fasten off.

Shape Armhole

Skip first 7 [7, 7, 9, 9, 9] sts. Rejoin yarn with a sl st to next st.

Row 1: Ch 1, sc in same st as sl st, *dc in next st, sc in next st; repeat from * across leaving the remaining 7 [7, 7, 9, 9, 9] sts unworked, turn. (53 [57, 61, 63, 69, 75] sts)

Rows 2-4: *(3 rows)* Ch 1, sc2tog, dc in next st, *sc in next st, dc in next st; repeat from * across until 2 sts remain, sc2tog, turn.

Row 5: Ch 3, *sc in next st, dc in next st; repeat from * across, turn. (47 [51, 55, 57, 63, 69] sts)

Row 6: Ch 1, sc in first st,*dc in next st, sc in next st; repeat from * across, turn.

Repeat Rows 5-6 until you have completed a total of 34 [36, 38, 38, 42, 42] rows.

Fasten off.

FRONT PANEL

Bottom Ribbing

Ch 9

Row 1: Repeat Row 1 of Back Panel.

Row 2: Repeat Row 2 of Back Panel.

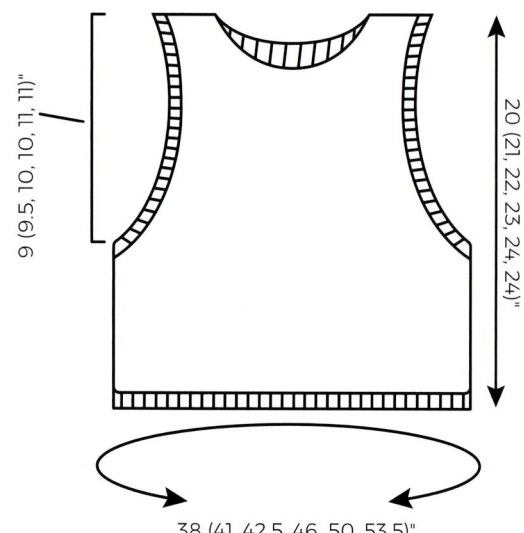

38 (41, 42.5, 46, 50, 53.5)"

Repeat Row 2 until you have completed a total of 67 [71, 75, 81, 87, 93] rows.

Turn to work into row ends.

Body

Row 1: Repeat Row 1 of Back Panel.

Row 2: Repeat Row 2 of Back Panel.

Row 3: Repeat Row 3 of Back Panel.

Repeat Rows 2-3 until you have completed a total of 33 [35, 37, 39, 41, 43] rows.

Fasten off.

Shape Armhole

Skip first 7 [7, 7, 9, 9, 9] sts. Rejoin yarn with a sl st to next st.

Rows 1-6: *(6 rows)* Repeat Rows 1-6 of Shape Armhole from Back Panel.

Repeat Rows 5-6 until you have completed a total of 26 [28, 30, 30, 34, 34] rows.

Do NOT fasten off. Continue to shoulder shaping.

Shoulder 1

Row 1: Ch 3, [sc in next st, dc in next st] 3 [4, 5, 6, 7, 8] times, turn. (7 [9, 11, 13, 15, 17] sts)

Row 2: Ch 1, sc in first st, *dc in next st, sc in next st; repeat from * across, turn.

Repeat Rows 1-2 until you have completed a total of 8 rows. Fasten off.

Shoulder 2

With the right side facing rejoin yarn to the 7 [9, 11, 13, 15, 17] th st from the edge.

Rows 1-2: *(2 rows)* Repeat Row 1-2 of Shoulder 1.

Repeat Rows 1-2 until you have completed a total of 8 rows. Fasten off.

ASSEMBLY

Joining Panels

With right sides touching, lay the front panel on back panel, lining up shoulder seam of front panel with corresponding stitches of back panel. Using tapestry needle and tail, seam the shoulders together using a whip stitch, making sure not to seam armholes.

Seaming Sides

Using tapestry needle and tail, seam the sides of front and back panels together, leaving a 7 ½ [8, 8, 8 ½, 9, 9]" / 19 [20, 20, 21.5, 23, 23] cm opening for armholes.

ARMHOLE RIBBING

With right side facing, join yarn at the underarm seam with a sl st.

Set-Up Round: Ch 1, sc evenly around the entire armhole, sl st to the first sc to join.

Ch 5

Row 1: Sc in second ch from hook and in each ch across, sl st in each of next 2 sts from Set-Up Round, turn. (4 sc)

Row 2: Do NOT ch; skip first 2 sl sts; working in **back loops** only, sc in each st across, turn.

Row 3: Ch 1; working in **back loops** only, sc in each st across; sl st in next 2 sts from set-up round, turn.

Repeat Rows 2-3 until you have created the ribbing around the entire Set-Up Round. Fasten off, leaving a long tail for sewing. Using tapestry needle and tail, sew the first row to the last row. Weave in ends.

NECKLINE RIBBING

With right side facing, join yarn to neckline with a sl st at one of the shoulder seams.

Set-Up Round: Ch 1, sc evenly around the entire neckline, sl st to the first sc to join

Ch 5

Row 1: Sc in second ch from hook and in each ch across, sl st in each of next 2 sts from Set-Up Round, turn. (4 sc)

Row 2: Do not ch; skip first 2 sl sts; working in **back loops** only, sc in each st across, turn.

Row 3: Ch 1; working in **back loops** only, sc in each st across; sl st in next 2 sts from Set-Up Round, turn.

Repeat Rows 2-3 until you have created the ribbing around the entire Set-Up Round. Fasten off, leaving a long tail for sewing. Using tapestry needle and tail, sew the first row to the last row. Weave in ends.

NEWBRIDGE
TURTLENECK SLIPOVER

This slipover features a cozy turtleneck and ribbed detailing around the armholes, creating a polished yet casual look. Ideal for layering over shirts or dresses.

SKILL LEVEL
Intermediate

LIST OF MATERIALS
Drops, Nepal – Dark Grey (0506)
(1.8 oz, 82 yds / 50 g, 75 m);
10 [10, 11, 11, 12, 13] balls

Size I-9 (5.5 mm) hook

Tapestry Needle

GAUGE
14 sts = 4" (10 cm); 12 rows = 4" (10 cm)

ABBREVIATIONS
st: stitch
ch: chain
hhdc: herringbone half double crochet
hhdc2tog: herringbone half double crochet 2 together
sc: single crochet
sl st: slip stitch

SIZING

Instructions given for Small, with changes for Medium, Large, XL, 2XL, 3XL are in [ ].

SIZE	S	M	L	XL	2XL	3XL
Finished Bust	42" 107 cm	45" 114 cm	47" 119 cm	50" 127 cm	55" 140 cm	58" 147 cm
Length	22" 56 cm	22" 56 cm	23" 58.5 cm	23" 58.5 cm	24" 61 cm	25" 63.5 cm

Special Stitches

Herringbone Half Double Crochet (hhdc): yo, insert hook into next st indicated, yo, pull up a loop and pull directly through first loop on hook, yo, draw through remaining two loops on hook.

Herringbone Half Double Crochet 2 Together (hhdc2tog): [yo, insert hook into next st indicated, pull up a loop and pull directly through first loop on hook] twice, *(3 loops on hook)*, yo, draw through remaining loops on hook.

Pattern Notes

Ch 1 at beginning of row does NOT count as first stitch

BACK PANEL

Bottom Hemline

Ch 13 (All sizes)

Row 1: Sc in second ch from hook and in each ch across, turn. (12 sc)

Row 2: Ch 1; working in **back loops** only, sc in each st across, turn.

Repeat Row 2 until you have a total of 74 [78, 82, 88, 96, 102] rows.

Turn to work into row ends.

Body

Row 1: *(Right Side)* Ch 1, hhdc in each row end, turn. (74 [78, 82, 88, 96, 102] hdc)

Row 2: Ch 1, hhdc in each st across, turn.

Repeat Row 2 until you have a total of 28 [28, 30, 30, 30, 34] rows.

Fasten off.

ARMHOLE SHAPING

With the right side facing, skip first 7 [7, 7, 9, 9, 10] sts. Join yarn with sl st to next st.

Row 1: *(Right Side)* Ch 1, hhdc in each of next 60 [64, 68, 70, 78, 82] sts, leaving remaining 7 [7, 7, 9, 9, 10] sts unworked, turn. (60 [64, 68, 70, 78, 82] hhdc)

Rows 2-4: *(3 rows)* Ch 1, hhdc2tog, hhdc in each st across until 2 sts remain, hhdc2tog, turn. (54 [58, 62, 64, 72, 76] hhdc)

Row 5: Ch 1, hhdc in each st across, turn.

Rows 6-40 [40, 40, 42, 42, 42]: *(35 [35, 35, 37, 37, 37] rows)* Repeat Row 5.

Fasten off.

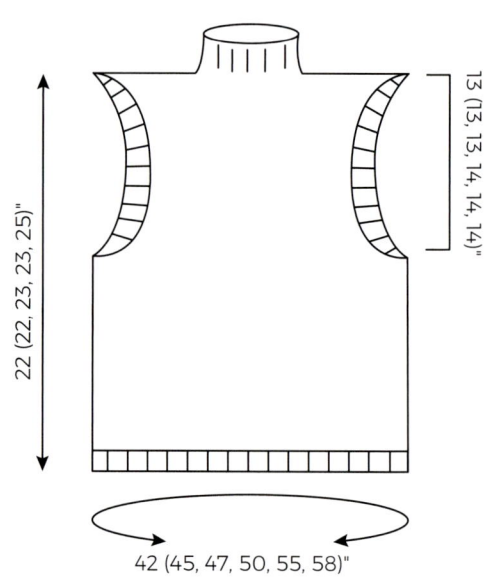

66

FRONT PANEL

Ribbed Hem

Repeat as for Ribbed Hem of Back Panel.

Turn to work into row ends.

Body

Rows 1-4: *(4 rows)* Repeat Rows 1-4 for Body of Back Panel.

Rows 5-62 [62, 64, 66, 66, 70]: *(58 [58, 60, 62, 62, 66] rows)* Repeat Row 5.

SHAPE LEFT NECK

Row 1: Ch 1, hhdc in next 16 [18, 20, 21, 25, 26] sts, turn.

Row 2: Ch 1, hhdc2tog, hhdc in each st across, turn. (15 [17, 19, 20, 24, 25] hhdc)

Rows 5-6: *(2 rows)* Repeat Rows 3 and 4. (11 [13, 15, 16, 20, 21] hhdc)

Fasten off, leaving a long tail for sewing.

ASSEMBLY

Joining Panels

Lay front panel on back panel, lining up edges of row ends. Using tapestry needle and tail, seam each side of front panel through both layers using a whip stitch. Do NOT seam armhole opening.

Joining Sholder Seams

Using tapestry needle and tail, seam the shoulder seams together with a whip stitch.

COLLAR

Ch 35 (All sizes)

Row 1: Sc in second ch from the hook and in each ch across, turn. [24 sc]

Row 2: Ch 1; working in **back loops** only, sc in each st across, turn.

Repeat Row 2 until fabric measures 18" (46 cm). Join short edges together and sc across to seam.

Fasten off, leaving a long tail for sewing. Using tapestry needle and tail, sew the collar to neck opening with a whip stitch.

ARMHOLE RIBBING

Join yarn at the underarm seam.

Set-up Round: Ch 1, sc evenly into each row end of armhole, sl st to beginning sc to join, turn.

Row 1: Ch 6, sc in second ch from hook and in each ch across, sl st in each of next 2 sts from Set-Up Round, turn. (5 sc)

Row 2: Do not ch, skip 2 sl sts just made; working in **back loops** only, sc in each of next 4 sts, sc in last st, turn.

Row 3: Ch 1, sc in first st; working in **back loops** only, sc in each of next 4 sts, sl st in each of next 2 sts from Set-Up Round, turn.

Repeat Rows 2-3 until you have created the ribbing around the entire Set-Up Round. Fasten off, leaving a long tail. Using tapestry needle and tail, seam first and last row together using a whip stitch. Repeat process for second armhole.

Weave in all ends.

NEWPORT TOP DOWN SWEATER

A crochet raglan, or top-down sweater, offers a comfortable, casual fit with its signature diagonal seam sleeves that extend from the neckline. This versatile design allows for easy customization of fit and color, making it a popular choice for everyday wear. Perfect for layering, it's a stylish and practical wardrobe staple.

SKILL LEVEL

Intermediate

LIST OF MATERIALS

Lion Brand, Jeans – Top Stitch
(3 ½ oz, 246 yds / 100 g, 225 m);
5 [6, 6, 7, 7, 8] balls

Size H-8 (5 mm) hook

Size J-10 (6 mm) hook

Tapestry Needle

GAUGE

16 sts = 4" (10 cm); 19 rows = 4" (10 cm)

ABBREVIATIONS

ch: chain
ch-2 sp: chain 2 space
hdc: half double crochet
sc: single crochet
sc2tog: single crochet 2 together
sl st: slip stitch
sp: space
st(s): stitch(es)

SIZING

Instructions given for Small, with changes for Medium, Large, XL, 2XL, 3XL are in [ ].

SIZE	S	M	L	XL	2XL	3XL
Finished bust	42" 107 cm	45" 114 cm	47" 119 cm	50" 127 cm	55" 140 cm	58" 147 cm
Length	22" 56 cm	22" 56 cm	23" 58.5 cm	23" 58.5 cm	24" 61 cm	25" 63.5 cm

Special Stitches

Single Crochet 2 Together (sc2tog): [Insert hook in next st or sp indicated and pull up a loop] twice, *(three lps on hook)*, yo, draw through all loops on hook.

Pattern Notes

Ch 1 at beginning of row does NOT count as first stitch

COLLAR

Using Size H-8 (5 mm) hook

Ch 8

Row 1: Sc in second ch from hook and in each ch across, turn. (7 sc)

Row 2: Ch 1; working in **back loops** only, sc in each st across, turn.

Rows 3-84: *(82 rows)* Repeat Row 2.

Do not fasten off. Sl st the first and last rows together. Turn the collar so the seam is in the inside.

Turn to work into row ends.

YOKE

Using Size H-8 (5 mm) hook

Set-Up Round: Ch 1, sc in each of the next 84 row ends, turn. (84 sc)

Round 1: Ch 1, hdc in each of the next 12 sts, (hdc, ch 2, hdc) in next st, hdc in each of next 16 sts, (hdc, ch 2, hdc) in next st, hdc in each of next 24 sts, (hdc, ch 2, hdc) in next st, hdc in each of next 16 sts, (hdc, ch 2, hdc) in next st, hdc in each of next 12 sts, sl st to first hdc to join, turn. (88 hdc)

Round 2: Ch 1, [hdc in each st to next ch-2 sp, (hdc, ch 2, hdc) in ch-2 sp] 4 times, hdc in each st around, sl st to first hdc to join, turn. (96 hdc)

Repeat Round 2 until you have completed a total of 18 [20, 22, 24, 26, 30] rounds, for a total of 224 [240, 256, 272, 288, 320] sts

SEPARATE BODY and SLEEVES

Set-Up: Ch 1, [hdc in each st to next ch-2 sp, work 1 hdc in ch-2 sp, skip each of next 50 [54, 58, 62, 66, 74] sts, work 1 hdc in next ch-2 sp] 2 times, hdc in each st around, sl st to first hdc to join, turn.

BODY

Round 1: Ch 1, hdc in each st around, sl st to first hdc to join, turn.

Repeat Round 1 until you have completed a total of 30 [32, 34, 34, 36, 36] rounds. Do NOT fasten off. Continue to bottom ribbing.

BOTTOM RIBBING

Ch 8

Row 1: Sc in second ch from hook and in each of next 7 ch, sl st in each of next 2 sts from body of sweater, turn. (7 sc)

Row 2: Do NOT ch; skip first 2 sl sts; working in **back**

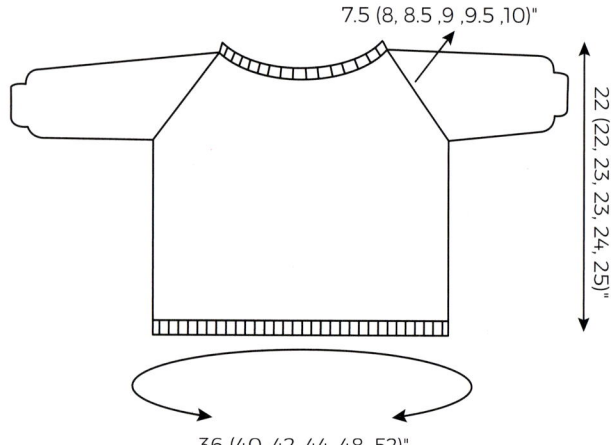

7.5 (8, 8.5, 9, 9.5, 10)"

22 (22, 23, 23, 24, 25)"

36 (40, 42, 44, 48, 52)"

loops only, sc in each st across, turn.

Row 3: Ch 1; working in **back loops** only, sc in each of next 7 sts; sl st in next 2 sts from body of sweater, turn.

Repeat Rows 2-3 until you have created the ribbing around the entire bottom edge of sweater. Fasten off, leaving a long tail for sewing. Using tapestry needle and tail, sew the first row to the last row. Weave in ends.

SLEEVES (Make 2)

Join yarn with sl st to ch-2 sp at the underarm.

Round 1: Ch 1, hdc in same st as join, hdc in each st to next ch-2 sp, hdc in next ch-2 sp, hdc in sp between last 2 sts, sl st in first hdc to join, turn.

Rounds 2-40: *(39 rounds)* Ch 1, hdc in each st around, turn.

Round 41: Ch 1, *sc2tog; repeat * around, turn. Do not fasten off. Continue to cuff.

CUFF (Make 2)

Set-Up Round: Ch 1, sc in each st around.

Sl st to the first sc to join.

Ch 7

Row 1: Sc in second ch from hook and in each ch across, sl st in each of next 2 sts from Set-Up Round, turn. (6 sc)

Row 2: Do not ch; skip first 2 sl sts; working in **back loops** only, sc in each st across, turn.

Row 3: Ch 1, sc in first st; working in **back loops** only, sc in each of next 6 sts; sl st in next 2 sts from Set-Up Round, turn.

Repeat Rows 2-3 until you have created the ribbing around the entire Set-Up Round.

Fasten off, leaving a long tail for sewing. Using tapestry needle and tail, sew the first row to the last row. Weave in ends.

OMEY PUFFY SWEATER

This lightweight puff stitch sweater features a classic round neck and subtle balloon sleeves, blending comfort with playful texture. The airy design makes it perfect for milder weather, while the puff stitch adds dimension and charm. Its stylish silhouette offers a trendy yet timeless addition to any wardrobe.

SKILL LEVEL

Intermediate

LIST OF MATERIALS

Drops, Flora – White Fog
(1 ¾ oz, 230 yds / 50 g, 210 m);
10 [10, 11, 11, 12, 12] balls

Size F-5 (3.75 mm) hook

Size C-2 (2.75 mm) hook

Tapestry Needle

GAUGE

18 sts = 4" (10 cm); 17 rows = 4" (10 cm)

ABBREVIATIONS

ch: chain
hdc: half double crochet
ps: puff stitch
sc: single crochet
sl st: slip stitch
st(s): stitch(es)

SIZING

Instructions given for Small, with changes for Medium, Large, XL, 2XL, 3XL are in [ ].

SIZE	S	M	L	XL	2XL	3XL
Finished Bust	40" 107 cm	44" 112 cm	48" 122 cm	52" 132 cm	56" 142 cm	60" 152.5 cm
Length	23" 58.5 cm	23" 58.5 cm	24" 61 cm	24" 61 cm	25" 63.5 cm	25" 63.5 cm
Upper Arm Circumference	15" 38 cm	16" 41 cm	16" 41 cm	16" 41 cm	17" 43 cm	17" 43 cm

Special Stitches

Puff Stitch (ps): [Yarn over, insert hook in next st or sp indicated and pull up a loop] 4 times, *(nine lps on hook)*, yo, draw through all loops on hook.

Pattern Notes

Ch 1 at beginning of row does NOT count as first stitch

BACK PANEL

Using Size F-5 (3.75 mm) hook

Bottom Ribbing

Ch 13

Row 1: Hdc in second ch from hook and in each ch across, turn. (12 hdc)

Row 2: Ch 1, working in **back loops** only, hdc in each st across, turn.

Repeat Row 2 until you have completed 60 [66, 72, 78, 84, 90] rows.

Turn to work into row ends.

Body

Row 1: Ch 1, hdc in each of next 91 [99, 109, 117, 127, 135] row ends, turn.

Rows 2-3: *(2 rows)* Ch 1, hdc in each st across, turn.

Row 4: Ch 1, sc in first st, *ps in next st, sc in next st; repeat from * across, turn.

Rows 5-7: *(2 rows)* Ch 1, hdc in each st across, turn

Repeat Rows 4-7 until you have completed 87 [87, 91, 91, 95, 95] rows.

Fasten off.

FRONT PANEL

Using Size F-5 (3.75 mm) hook

Bottom Ribbing

Ch 13

Rows 1-2: *(2 rows)* Repeat Rows 1-2 of Bottom Ribbing for Back Panel

Repeat Row 2 until you have completed 60 [66, 72, 78, 84, 90] rows.

Turn to work into row ends.

Body

Rows 1-7: *(7 rows)* Repeat Rows 1-7 of Body for Back Panel

Repeat Rows 4-7 until you have completed 76 [76, 80, 80, 84, 84] rows, ending on a Row 4 Repeat. Do NOT fasten off. Continue to shoulder shaping.

Shoulder 1

Row 1: Ch 1, hdc in each of next 25 [29, 33, 39, 43, 47] sts, leaving remaining sts unworked, turn.

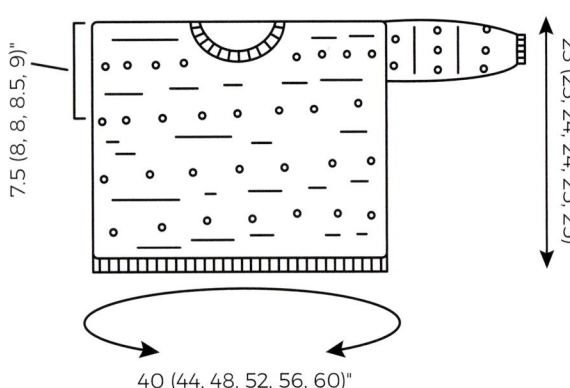

7.5 (8, 8, 8.5, 9)"

23 (23, 24, 24, 25, 25)"

40 (44, 48, 52, 56, 60)"

Rows 2-3: *(2 rows)* Ch 1, hdc in each st across, turn.

Row 4: Ch 1, sc in first st, *ps in next st, sc in next st; repeat from * across, turn

Rows 5-7: *(3 rows)* Ch 1, hdc in each st across, turn.

Repeat Rows 4-7 one more time for a total of 11 rows.

Fasten off

Shoulder 2

With the right side facing rejoin yarn to the 25 [29, 33, 39, 43, 47]th st from the edge.

Rows 1-2: *(2 rows)* Repeat Rows 1-2 of Shoulder 1.

Repeat Rows 4-7 one more time for a total of 11 rows.

Fasten off

ASSEMBLY

Joining Panels

With right sides together, lay the front panel on back panel, lining row up shoulder seam. Using tapestry needle and tail, seam the shoulders together using a whip stitch.

Seaming Sides

Using tapestry needle and tail, seam the sides of front and back panels together, leaving a 7 ½ [8, 8, 8, 8 ½, 9]" / 19 [20, 20, 20, 21.5, 23] cm opening for sleeves.

SLEEVES (Make 2)

With right side facing, join yarn with a sl st to underarm seam.

Round 1: Ch 1, hdc in each of of next 68 [72, 72, 72, 76, 76] sts around the opening, sl st to first hdc to join, turn.

Rounds 2-3: *(2 rounds)* Ch 1, hdc in each st around, turn.

Round 4: Ch 1, *sc in next st, ps in next st; repeat from * around, turn.

Rounds 5-7: *(3 rounds)* Ch 1, hdc in each st around, turn.

Repeat Rounds 4-7 until you have completed a total of 67 rounds. Do not fasten off. Continue to cuff.

CUFF (Make 2)

Using Size C-2 (2.75 mm) hook

Ch 8

Row 1: Hdc in second ch from hook and in each ch across, sl st in each of next 2 sts from main sleeve body, turn. (7 hdc)

Row 2: Do not ch; skip first 2 sl sts; working in **back loops** only, hdc in each across, turn.

Row 3: Ch 1; working in **back loops** only, hdc in each of next 7 sts; sl st in next 2 sts from main sleeve body, turn.

Repeat Rows 2-3 until you have created the ribbing around the entire sleeve. Fasten off, leaving a long tail for sewing. Using tapestry needle and tail, sew the first row to the last row. Weave in ends.

NECKLINE RIBBING

Using Size F-5 (3.75 mm) hook

With right side facing, join yarn to neckline with a sl st at one of the shoulder seams.

Set-Up Round: Ch 1, sc evenly around the entire neckline, sl st to the first sc to join.

Ch 6

Row 1: Hdc in second ch from hook and in each ch across, sl st in each of next 2 sts from Set-Up Round, turn. (5 sc)

Row 2: Do not ch; skip first 2 sl sts; working in **back loops** only, hdc in each st across, turn.

Row 3: Ch 1; working in **back loops** only, hdc in each st across; sl st in next 2 sts from Set-Up Round, turn.

Repeat Rows 2-3 until you have created the ribbing around the entire set-up round. Fasten off, leaving a long tail for sewing. Using tapestry needle and tail, sew the first row to the last row. Weave in ends.

ROUNDSTONE
COCOON SHRUG

This shrug adds a chic and cozy layer to any outfit, featuring a beautiful, eye-catching stitch texture. This versatile piece is perfect for transitioning between seasons, offering warmth and style.

SKILL LEVEL
Intermediate

LIST OF MATERIALS
Patons, Wool Blend Aran – Grey
(4 oz, 202 yds / 100 g, 185 m);
6 (7, 7) balls

Size J-10 (6 mm) hook

Stitch Markers

Tapestry Needle

GAUGE
12 sts = 4" (10 cm); 11 rows = 4" (10 cm)

ABBREVIATIONS
ch: chain
dc: double crochet
FPtr: front post treble crochet
sc: single crochet
sl st: slip stitch
st(s): stitch(es)

SIZING

Instructions given for Small/Medium, with changes for Large/XL and 2XL/3XL are in [ ].

SIZE	S/M	L/XL	2XL/3XL
Width	34" 86 cm	40" 101.5 cm	46" 117 cm
Length	26" 66 cm	28" 71 cm	30" 76 cm

Pattern Notes

Ch 2 at the beginning of a row does count as the first stitch.

Ch 1 at beginning of row does NOT count as first stitch

BODY

Leaving a long tail, ch 104 [122, 140]

Row 1: *(Right Side)* dc in third ch from hook and in each ch across, turn. (103 [121, 139] dc)

Row 2: Ch 1, sc in each st across, turn.

Row 3: Ch 2, *FPtr in next dc 2 rows below, dc in next sc; repeat from * across, turn.

Row 4: Repeat Row 2.

Row 5: Ch 2, dc in next sc, *FPtr in next dc 2 rows below, dc in next sc; repeat from * across, dc in last sc, turn.

Row 6: Repeat Row 2.

Rows 7-70 [78, 82]: *(64 [72, 76] rows)* Repeat Rows 3-6.

Fasten off, leaving a long tail for seaming. Block to measurements.

CREATING ARM HOLES

Lay body flat with right side facing. Fold fabric in half width wise, so that the first row and final row line up. You can use locking stitch markers along the side seams to hold in place.

Place a stitch marker 5 ½ [5 ½, 6]" (14 [14,15] cm) in from the folded crease on each side creating armholes.

Using a tapestry needle and tail, seam both layers of fabric together, working from the folded corner to the stitch marker. Fasten off. Repeat for opposite armhole.

COLLAR RIBBING

Turn your piece right side out and lay your work out so it resembles a diamond. Rejoin yarn with a sl st at one of the armhole seams.

Set-Up Round: Ch 1, sc in each st around entire inner edge, sl st in first sc to join.

Ch 13

Row 1: Sc in second ch from hook and in each ch across, sl st in each of next 2 sts from Set-Up Round, turn. (12 sc)

Row 2: Do not ch; skip first 2 sl sts; working in **back loops** only, sc in each of next 11 sts, sc in last st, turn.

Row 3: Ch 1, sc in first st; working in **back loops** only, sc in each of next 11 sts, sl st in next 2 sts from Set-Up Round, turn.

Repeat Rows 2-3 until you have created the ribbing around the entire set-up round. Fasten off, leaving a long tail. Using tapestry needle and tail, seam first and last row together using a whip stitch. Weave in ends.

SLEEVES (Make 2)

Ch 35

Row 1: Sc in second ch from hook and in each ch across, turn. (34 sc)

Row 2: Ch 1, sc in first st; working in **back loops** only, sc in each of next 32 sts, sc in last st, turn.
Repeat Row 2 until you have a total of 34 [34, 36] rows.

Fold fabric in half width wise, so the first row and final row line up. Ch 1, sl st through both layers of fabric to seam. Fasten off, leaving a long tail for seaming to the body.

ATTACHING SLEEVES

Turn body of cardigan wrong side out. Using tapestry needle and tail, seam sleeves to armholes. Weave in remaining ends.

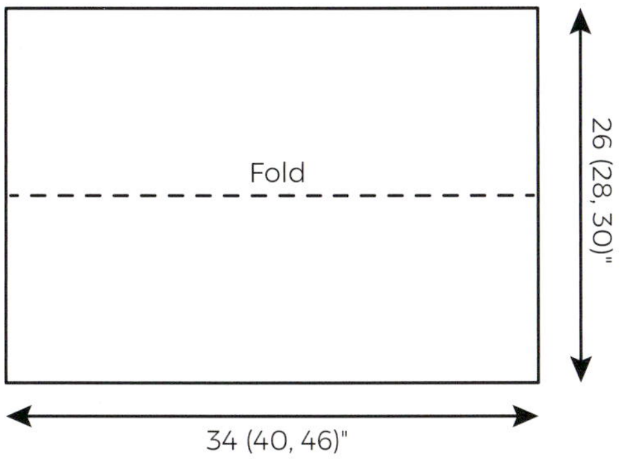

26 (28, 30)"

Fold

34 (40, 46)"

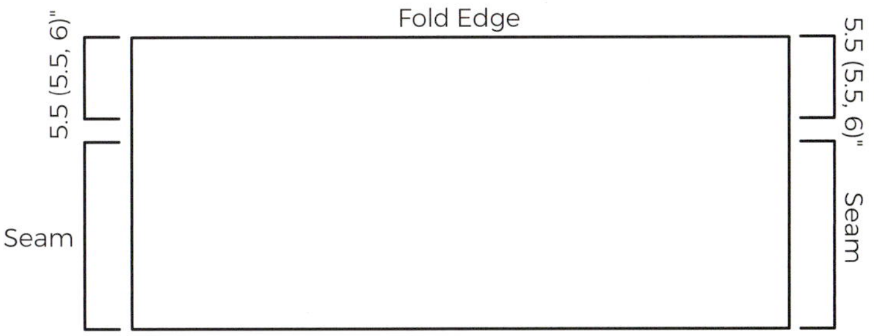

Fold Edge

5.5 (5.5, 6)"

5.5 (5.5, 6)"

Seam

Seam

85

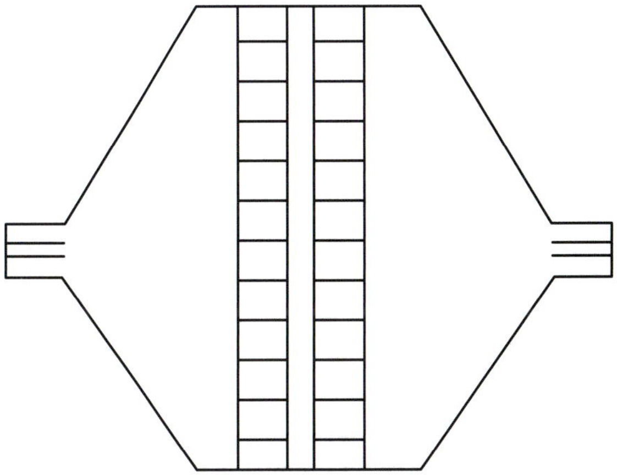

MULRANNY
SWEATER

This lightweight sweater is constructed from two T-shaped panels, offering a quick and easy design. Featuring a wide boat neck, it drapes beautifully for a relaxed fit. The simple yet stylish construction makes it ideal for beginners, while still creating a chic, versatile wardrobe staple.

SKILL LEVEL

Intermediate

LIST OF MATERIALS

Hobbii, Friends Cotton 8/4 – Whisky
(1 ¾ oz, 174 yds / 50g, 160 m);
9 [10, 10, 11, 11, 12] balls

Size F-5 (3.75 mm) hook

Tapestry Needle

GAUGE

16 sts = 4" (10 cm); 19 rows = 4" (10 cm)

ABBREVIATIONS

ch: chain
dc: double crochet
sc: single crochet
sl st: slip stitch
st(s): stitch(es)

SIZING

Instructions given for Small, with changes for Medium, Large, XL, 2XL, 3XL are in [ ].

SIZE	S	M	L	XL	2XL	3XL
Finished Bust	38" 96.5 cm	40" 102 cm	42" 107 cm	46" 117 cm	50" 127 cm	54" 137 cm
Total Length	19" 48 cm	20" 51 cm	21" 53 cm	22" 56 cm	23" 58.5 cm	24" 61 cm
Arm Circumference	15" 38 cm	16" 41 cm	16" 41 cm	17" 43 cm	17" 43 cm	18" 46 cm
Neck Opening	8" 20 cm	8" 20 cm	8" 20 cm	8.5" 21.5 cm	9" 23 cm	9" 23 cm

Pattern Notes

Ch 1 at beginning of row does NOT count as first stitch.

Ch 3 at beginning of row does count as first stitch.

PANELS (Make 2)

Leaving a long tail for seaming, Foundation sc 77 [81, 85, 93, 101, 109]

Row 1: Ch 1, sc in first st, *dc in next st, sc in next st; repeat from * across, turn.

Row 2: Ch 3, *sc in next st, dc in next st; repeat from * across, turn.

Repeat Rows 1-2 until the you have completed a total of 54 [58, 62, 64, 70, 72].

Do not fasten off.

SLEEVES/BODY

With a new ball of yarn join to the top left side with a sl st, ch 68 and fasten off. This sets up the left sleeve.

Using working yarn from front panel,

Row 1: Ch 69, sc in second ch from hook, *dc in next ch, sc in next ch; repeat from * across, repeat from * across front panel; repeat from * across each ch from left sleeve, turn. (213 [217, 221, 229, 237, 245] sts)

Row 2: Ch 3, *sc in next st, dc in the next; repeat from * across, turn.

Row 3: Ch 1, sc in first st, *dc in next st, sc in next st; repeat from * across, turn.

Repeat Rows 2-3 until you have completed a total of 35 [37, 37, 39, 39, 43].

Fasten off.

ASSEMBLY

Joining Panels and Bottom of Sleeves

With right sides facing, lay the front panel on back panel, lining up row ends. Using tapestry needle and long tail, seam the panels and bottom of sleeves together using a whip stitch.

Joining Sleeve Seams and Shoulder

Lining up row ends and starting at end of sleeve, seam sleeves together using tapestry needle and long tail. Seam shoulder seam together, leaving a large neck opening.

Weave in ends.

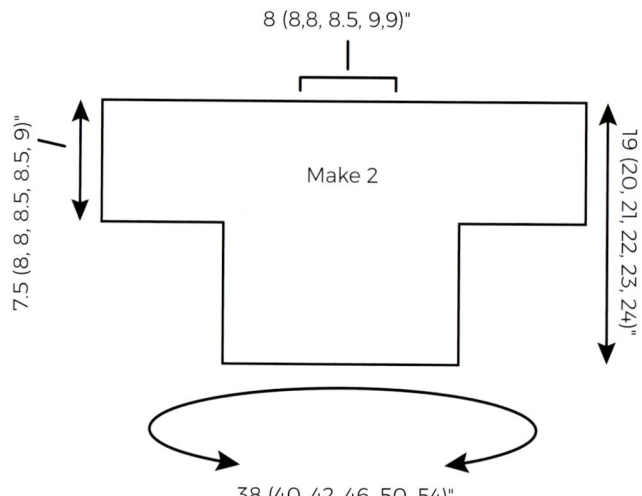

SYCAMORE
HOODED GILET

A hooded gilet made from faux fur yarn combines luxurious texture with practical warmth. This sleeveless gilet is perfect for layering in colder month and the cozy hood adds extra comfort. Its plush faux fur yarn adds a chic, modern twist to a classic piece.

SKILL LEVEL
Intermediate

LIST OF MATERIALS
Sirdar Alpine, Faux Fur – Brindle
(1 ¾ oz, 36 yds / 50 g, 33 m);
12 [13, 13, 14, 15, 15] balls

Size 12 mm hook

Tapestry Needle

GAUGE
6 sts = 4" (10 cm); 7 rows = 4" (10 cm)

ABBREVIATIONS
ch: chain
sc: single crochet
sc2tog: single crochet 2 together
st(s): stitch(es)

SIZING

Instructions given for Small, with changes for Medium, Large, XL, 2XL, 3XL are in [ ].

SIZE	S	M	L	XL	2XL	3XL
Finished bust	32" 81 cm	36" 91.5 cm	40" 101.5 cm	44" 112 cm	48" 122 cm	52" 132 cm
Shoulder to shoulder	16" 40.5 cm	18" 46 cm	20" 51 cm	22" 56 cm	24" 61 cm	26" 66 cm
Length	17" 43 cm	18" 46 cm	18" 46 cm	19" 48 cm	20" 51 cm	21" 53 cm

Pattern Notes

Ch 1 at beginning of row does NOT count as first stitch

BACK PANEL

Ch 25 [28, 31, 34, 37, 40]

Row 1: Sc in second ch from the hook and in each ch across, turn. (24 [27, 30, 33, 36, 39] sc)

Row 2: Ch 1, sc in each st across, turn.

Repeat Row 2 until you have completed a total of 30 [32, 32, 34, 36, 38] rows. Fasten off.

FRONT PANEL (Make 2)

Ch 16 [18, 19, 21, 22, 23]

Row 1: Repeat Row 1 of Back Panel. (15 [17, 18, 20, 21, 22] sc)

Row 2: Repeat Row 2 of Back Panel

Repeat Row 2 until you have completed a total of 30 [32, 32, 34, 36, 38] rows. Fasten off, leaving a long tail.

HOOD (Make 2)

Ch 14 [15, 16, 17, 18, 19]

Row 1: Repeat Row 1 of Back Panel (13 [14, 15, 16, 17, 18] sc)

Rows 2-18: *(17 rows)* Repeat Row 2 of Back Panel.

Row 19: Ch 1, sc in each st across until 2 sts remain, sc2tog, turn. (12 [13, 14, 15, 16, 17] sc)

Row 20: Ch 1, sc2tog, sc in each st across, turn. (11 [12, 13, 14, 15, 16] sc)

Row 21: Repeat Row 19 (10 [11, 12, 13, 14, 15] sc).

Row 22: Repeat Row 20. (9 [10, 11, 12, 13, 14] sc).

Fasten off, leaving a long tail.

ASSEMBLY

Joining Panels

Lay the front panels on back panel, lining up shoulder seams. Using tapestry needle and tail, seam the shoulders together using a whip stitch across 7 [8, 9, 10, 11, 11] sts.

Seaming Sides

Using tapestry needle and tail, seam the sides of front and back panels together, leaving a 8 [8, 8 ½, 9, 9, 9 ½]" / 19 [19, 21.5, 23, 23, 24] cm opening for armholes.

Joining Hood

Lay hood panels on top of one another and sew along the curved edge.

Turn the body right side out. Align bottom edge of hood with front and back panels of body, using stitch markers to hold in place. Using tapestry needle and tail, seam hood to body using a whip stitch.

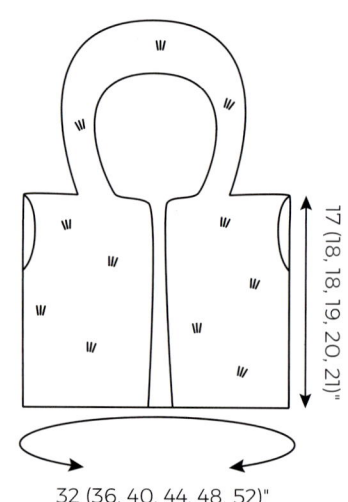

17 (18, 18, 19, 20, 21)"

32 (36, 40, 44, 48, 52)"

Edging

Rejoin yarn at the bottom corner of right front panel.

Rows 1-3: *(3 rows)* Ch 1, sc evenly around inner edging of right front panel, sc evenly around hood, sc evenly around inner edging of left front panel.

Fasten off. Weave in ends.